AF478201

Not So Savage

THE SAVAGE CLUB
LADIES DINNER.
Guests of the Club
Miss Lily Brayton. and Oscar Asche.
Tom Marlowe Esqr
in the chair
May 22nd 1909
Hotel Cecil
MENU
Sardines Anchois Salade Nicoise
Consommé Imperial
Crème Princesse
Darne de Saumon Sauce Crevettes
Salade de Concombres
Blanchaille Diable
Ris de Veau Toulouse
Selle d'Agneau à la Broche
Pommes Nouvelles Petits Pois
Sorbet au Crème de Menthe
Poularde en Casserole
Salade de Saison
Asperges sauce Mousseline
Poire Melba Glacée
Dessert
Café Noir.
WAR PAINT

Not So Savage

BY MATTHEW NORGATE
Chairman of the Arts Committee, Savage Club
AND ALAN WYKES
Honorary Secretary of the Savage Club

Jupiter Books · London

First published in 1976.
JUPITER BOOKS (LONDON) LIMITED
167 Hermitage Road, London N4 1LZ.

SBN 904041 271.

Set in 11/14pt Monotype Sabon 669 by
The Lancashire Typesetting Company Limited, Bolton.
Printed and bound by R. J. Acford Limited, Chichester.

Contents

George W. Whitelaw

Not So Savage

Savage Club
House Dinner
Saturday
January 27th 1917
Contributes at Poker
Plays Golf
Revokes at Bridge
TOM CLARE
In the Chair
Menu
Soup
Thick Mock Turtle
Steak, Kidney & Oyster Pudding
Sprouts   Potatoes
Compote of Fruit
Queen's Tartlets
Stilton Cheese — Celery

The 'I' in the text is Alan Wykes; the eye
that chose the pictures is Matthew Norgate's.

THE AUTHORS

Introduction

S AVAGE HOUSE DINNERS, like the club of which they form an integral and indispensable part, are unique. They have been imitated by other clubs in various parts of the world – and indeed by other clubs in London. To these last we shall raise our eyebrows and bow politely, recognizing that, in such cases, imitation is a worthy form of aspiration rather than of flattery; but being in this matter, if in no other, the snobbiest of the snobbish, we smile tolerantly and brush the speck of dust from our Rolls-Royce gleam. We are confident of our inimitability.

There are, I am told, people in the world who know what the Seven Deadly Sins, the Ten Commandments and similar trivia are, but know not what the Savage Club is, let alone what its House Dinners are. Although such benighted souls are scarcely to be credited, they must to some extent be pandered to; without such single-syllabled cosseting the book that lies in their hands (for which, one hopes, they have paid good money) will be, if not absolutely meaningless, at least baffling. One can hear them muttering in that phrase already ossified on the cold lips of antiquity – What's it all in aid of? It is in aid, my fine ossified friend, of those four words embedded in the Constitution of the United States: 'the pursuit of happiness'.

Thomas Jefferson was before us Savages, but not much. He died in 1826 and the Savage Club was born thirty-one years later – specifically, on Monday 12 October 1857. Gestation was short, for conception had

occurred only four days previously in a letter written by George Augustus
Sala, later a *Daily Telegraph* correspondent of distinction, the echo of
whose name still whispers round the walls of Fleet Street pubs. He was
young at the time – twenty-nine – and, so far as can be reliably established,
had discussed the formation of 'a Club of merry fellows' with one of the
founders of *Punch* – an artist called Ebenezer Landells. Since it is always
the secretary of anything who clutches at evanescent daydreams and hauls
them into the realms of practicality – *id est* does all the work – Sala
appointed himself Honorary Secretary *pro tem* and wrote to a suitable
number of merry fellows as follows:

Thursday, eighth October, 1857

Dear Sir,

The favour of your presence is requested at a meeting of gentlemen
connected with literature and the fine arts, and warmly interested in
the promotion of Christian knowledge, and the sale of exciseable
liquors to be holden at the Crown Tavern, Vinegar Yard, Drury Lane,
on Monday the 12th instant at five o'clock p.m. there and then to
confer upon the expediency of forming a social society or club,
hereafter to receive a suitable designation, and to have its *habitat*
at the Crown Tavern aforesaid.

I am Dear Sir
Yours very faithfully
George: aug: Sala
Hon: Sec: *pro: tem:*

Nobody knows how many men he sent the letter to; but the number
who turned up at the Crown on the 12th was quite small. (Perhaps the
opposing forces of Christian knowledge and exciseable liquors had to
some extent neutralized each other.) If the number was small, it is now
also indeterminable, for the minutes, if any, have disappeared; but many
who subsequently became Members claimed to have been at the founders'
meeting. Sala of course was there, so were Landells and the brothers
Brough – William and Robert – both of whom were dramatists. Andrew
Halliday was another journalist, and G. L. M. Strauss was a doctor.
He said that he thought the Club should include scientists. 'They will
give', he said, 'a leavening of seriousness into the Bohemian levity.'

There was no sign at that first meeting of anyone to do with music, which therefore remained, until 1956, when Law was roped somewhat tardily into the fold, the junior of the six categories of membership – Literature, Art, Drama, Science, Music, and Law. Members had, and still have, to present their credentials (through the auspices of their sponsors) as a professional in one of those fields of activity; and those credentials have to be minutely examined by an eighteen-strong Qualifications Committee whose business it is to see that no one, however wealthy or socially upstage, seizes the name Savage under the wire.

The naming of the Savage Club may be said to be both lost in the mists of antiquity and found in the shades of iniquity. Since no minutes of the first meeting survive, one can rely only on the two recorded stories: one, Sala's, that 'We dubbed ourselves Savages for mere fun'; the other, Dr Strauss's, that, having sought about for a name that would associate the club with the arts and many famous ones having been suggested and all found too grand, the name of Richard Savage was suddenly recalled. 'Just the thing', someone said. 'No one can say there's anything pretentious in *that* name.' As indeed there wasn't. Savage was an eighteenth-century minor poet who was given a sort of Civil List allowance of twenty pence a year for writing a birthday ode to Queen Caroline. He was also given the death sentence for killing a man in a drunken tavern brawl, but was pardoned after the intercession of one of the Queen's ladies-in-waiting, Lady Hertford. Like a later Savage, E. J. Odell, of whom more will be heard, he lived on the charity of his friends, but it wasn't sufficient for his dissolute habits of which he was finally 'cured' in a Bristol debtors' prison in 1743. This end made him a very suitable Godfather to a club which had a subscription described by one laconic Savage as 'just whatever the members choose to owe'.

The landlords of the several pubs where the Club met during the first ten years of its life were themselves charitable beyond the call of duty. They provided for the ordinary meetings of Savages a meal of bread and cheese, half a pint of porter, and a screw of tobacco – for fourpence. Saturdays were special – mainly because the journalistic week had ended and it was time for convivial relaxation – and rated a cold joint and a pie of some sort, plus wine and beer, at 'eightpence per Savage head' as the notice in the Lyceum Tavern, Strand, put it.

The Lyceum was the original venue of the House Dinner. In the absence
of a house, it wasn't of course called a House Dinner but a Saturday
Supper – or, occasionally and regrettably, a 'merrification'. (Even Savages
have their faults.) By that time – 1860 – the membership had increased
and the 'theatricals', as the Drama Members were invariably called,
arriving in the Club after their stint at the theatre, would discuss audience
and performance, giving imitative demonstrations of where and how their
fellow players had fluffed their lines or how the gallery had participated
uninvited. This of course led to reminiscence by other Savages present
and an embryo entertainment was established. Soon, singers were singing,
elecutionists were elocuting, artists were making graphic comments
on the performances on backs of envelopes, and writers and playwrights
were constructing monologues and sketches for the amusement of their
Saturday Supper companions.

In that Victorian decade, the London music-hall was at its zenith.
The Mogul or 'Old Mo' in Drury Lane (a few steps from the Lyceum
Tavern), the Canterbury, the Collins at Islington (named after the chimney
sweep who sang comic songs there), the Oxford, the Tivoli, and the
London Pavilion provided most of the available indoor public
entertainment. It served the purpose of television and wireless today;
and like many television programmes it made much use of an anchor-man.
The Chairman of these entertainments announced the artists in wildly
overstated terms ('at enormous expense'), encouraged the audience in their
applause, and filled in any unexpected gaps in the entertainment with
quips and comments.

It was a natural corollary of what was, after all, a music-hall type of
entertainment, that the Saturday Suppers should acquire an anchor-man
to 'call upon' (such was the idiom of the day) 'Brother Savage George
Grossmith to give us a recitation' – to give a typically distinguished
example. Performers simply stood up in their places if there was no
platform or piano to which they could gravitate. (In the early days there
often wasn't; in fact it was the search for better accommodation that
took the Club to nearly a dozen different homes during its early life.)
As at the music-hall, there was a continual to-ing and fro-ing, arriving
and departing – not only to replenish glasses but also to get to newspaper
offices with late stories or to the music-hall proper in time for one's call.

However, the informality, though unbridled in other respects, gradually became subject to one firmly established, if unwritten, rule: any performer indulging in undisguised coarseness was received with freezing silence.

Also received with a none-too-warm silence were requests for subscriptions. The Savage who said that the subscription was a matter for the individual debtor was laconically right. The main task of one early Honorary Treasurer, a Mr Tegetmeier, seems to have been first to pay the rent of the club room and any other incidental expenses out of his own pocket and then try and retrieve the money in the form of subscriptions if he could. He was either rich or selflessly dedicated, or possibly both, for he pursued this disinterested line of service for six years and then 'found another mug to hand over the reins to'. At the Saturday Supper marking his retirement he was presented with a microscope (presumably bought with money acquired in a whip-round). The speech accompanying the presentation moved, among other things, 'that this testimonial be presented to W. B. Tegetmeier for having for years past embezzled the funds of the Club' – an ungrateful resolution that was carried with acclamation. In this speech of acceptance he thanked Savages for the microscope, 'which will be of immeasurable value to me in my work as a naturalist'. He added drily that he was 'honoured to be Honorary and have had the privilege of paying out, over the years, some hundred and twenty pounds and receiving in return the sum of forty of the same in payment of subscriptions'.

The Executive of the Savage Club has always been Honorary in the truest sense. The books reveal nothing that could even remotely be called an honorarium, let alone a salary, being paid to any officer of the Executive – which, for the greater part of the Club's life, has numbered three: Secretary, Treasurer, and Solicitor. This being England, the scheme of things has always been democratic and an elected Committee also has to do with the running of the Club. (Democracy is theoretically a marvellous idea which doesn't work very efficiently as the parliamentary system so well attests.) To its Secretary, no Committee is heroic. He tends to think of it as suitable for designing camels but as an otherwise poor vehicle of progress – like the dedicatee of one of Wodehouse's novels, 'but for whom this book would have been finished a damn sight quicker'. Being unpaid, however, not only brings the pleasure of involvement in

GEORGE AUGUSTUS SALA

T. W. ROBERTSON

FOUR SAVAGE ANCESTORS

GEORGE CRUIKSHANK

DR. G. L. M. STRAUSS

policymaking, but also the deeper pleasure of being able to suggest a
good home for the Committee's more excessive demands.

Honorary Officers are elected annually, like the Committee, but
unlike Members of the Committee, they do not retire every third year.
This means that if they don't resign and no one offers to stand for
election in opposition, they remain in office for a very long time. Since
few want to undertake these jobs – which are time consuming and demand
gregariousness, diplomacy of an extreme degree, and understanding of
the nature of the Club and all its works – many Honorary Officers grow
white-haired in office.

The outstanding Honorary Secretary of the twentieth century was,
without doubt, George Baker, baritone singer and veteran recording artist
(he was recording in 1909). He was in office from 1938 to 1958 (having
done a seven-year stint as Honorary Treasurer before that), and by his
energy and devotion wound the Club up and kept it going, complete with
House Dinners (even though they were sometimes lunches), throughout
the difficult war years, even when its then home in Carlton House Terrace
was bombed. He perfectly expressed the civilized anarchy of the Savage
spirit in a contribution he made to the Centenary Dinner souvenir on
9 December 1957:

> What is a Savage? He is an uncompounded pill. Being an egoist, he
> hates egoism. Freedom of expression is his life's blood, therefore he
> dislikes people who have too much to say. He is suspicious of people
> who agree with him. He is a lover of joviality, but woe betide the
> man who gives himself a jovial welcome. He is a sentimentalist who
> hates sentiment. He is a man of affairs who scorns commercialism.
> As a Rabelaisian, he is unpredictably censorious. He is an
> unrepentant individualist, and for a hundred years Savages have
> been proving that freedom, not union, is strength, long before the
> politicians got on to the idea.

In the narrow political sense, Savages are of every hue, but the colour of
each is unrecognizable to all the others because politics, like religion, is
an unwelcome subject for conversation. No one cares what party flag his
vis-à-vis unfurls outside the Club doors. Equally, their private lives are
sealed off from any investigation on nomination. Place and date of birth,

education, wives, mistresses, influential friends, are as nothing in the
sight of the Qualifications Committee. The candidate may have done time
on the Siberian Gas Board or have access to the top-secret files of
The Elves, Gnomes, and Little Men's Science-Fiction, Marching, and
Chowder Society (I assure you there is a thus-named organization); but
if he isn't spiritually as well as professionally Savage he won't get in.

There was a time within my memory as Secretary when the financial
hazards of the future seemed to be as insuperable as those attending the
purchase of a Steinway with the money for a penny whistle (this taking
into consideration the fact that nowadays penny whistles cost thirty
pence). Over the horizon at that time loomed a millionaire with a
Rolls-Royce built round his telephone. He dearly wanted to become a
Savage and the rescue of the Club from its slough of despond was clearly
hinted at. But he wasn't qualified. End of story – though not, as you see,
of the Club, which rustled up its fortitude and pressed on as it had done
so many times before. Nothing is so jealously guarded as Savage
exclusiveness.

Paradoxically, there has always been an Honorary list by way of
which Royal Princes could be appointed Savages. (Monarchs are
constitutionally unable to be members of organizations.) This may appear
to be monstrously snobbish; but the link, as you will see in a moment,
is forged directly to the House Dinner.

The first Royal to be elected was Edward VII when he was Prince of
Wales; and that was in 1882, the year of the Club's twenty-fifth
anniversary. He said in response to the toast proposed by the Chairman,
Sir Philip Cunliffe-Owen:

Gentlemen, for the far too flattering manner in which my friend,
Sir Philip Cunliffe-Owen, has been kind enough to propose the
toast, and for the way in which you have received it, I beg to express
my most sincere and cordial thanks. I can assure you that I take it
as a very high compliment to have been invited here tonight, to
assist in celebrating the twenty-fifth anniversary of the existence of
your Club. I beg also to return my most sincere thanks for the
compliment you have paid me in asking me to become an honorary
member of the Savage Club. I cannot say how much pleasure it gives

me to do so. Though I have not been formally elected, the kind
way in which you have received me here gives me some hope that
you will offer no objection to my election.

In becoming a member of your Club I feel I am not among
strangers, for at this moment I can see around and before me many
gentlemen whom I have had the advantage of knowing, some in
distant parts of the Empire. Others there are who have made me
both laugh and cry. I am well aware that your Club consists of
gentlemen connected with literature, with art, with journalism, with
science, music, and with the drama, and I can easily understand how
you must enjoy these convivial meetings after the long and arduous
duties of your respective callings.

Gentlemen, I am given to understand that your qualifications are
that you must belong to literature and art, and also that you must
be good fellows. I feel that I can hardly aspire to the first
qualification in order to be a competent member; but if you will
allow me, I will be the second. Before knowing anything personally
about your Club I was asked of what it consisted, and one of my
nephews asked me what was meant by my going to dine with
savages. Now, according to the very pretty menu which I have before
me, and which has been executed by Mr Harry Furniss, one of your
members, the gentlemen belonging to the Savages wore light clothing.
After partaking of your kind hospitality tonight, and your reception
of me this evening, I shall be able to inform my nephew that you
are by no means the savages he might have imagined, but are as
civilized as any other gentlemen he may meet with. Although I do
not see you with those feathers depicted on the menu, still we are
all enjoying the pipe of peace.

As I know that many of you have to leave early, and there is still a
lengthy and most entertaining programme before us, I will not detain
you longer. Before, however, sitting down, I wish to propose a
toast, and so, with great pleasure, I propose 'Prosperity to the
Savage Club'. I have additional pleasure in coupling with it the
name of our Chairman, Sir Philip Cunliffe-Owen. He has been good
enough to make some too flattering allusions to the Exhibitions
both at Vienna and Paris, and all I can say is that, unless I had had

his great assistance and untiring energy on both occasions, those
Exhibitions, as far as the English portions were concerned, would
not have been the successes they were. I now, gentlemen, call upon
you to drink with me the health of the Chairman and Prosperity
to the Savage Club.

The newspapers, which in those days were not so ridden with
the diseases of doom and disaster, gave the event wide coverage. *The
Observer*, for example, even gave a run-down of the items in the
after-dinner entertainment:

The proceedings commenced with the performance of a march for
the piano by Messrs Theodore Drew and Charles Hargitt, a very
spirited piece of execution. Then came a run of actors who
contributed songs and recitations before they ran away to their
regular duties at the theatres. Thus, Mr Lionel Brough sang 'The

Muddle Puddle Porter' with exceeding unction, and Mr Paulton
followed with a droll burlesque lecture on 'Time'. Mr George
Grossmith next took off the peculiarities of the music-hall *comique*,
and Mr J. L. Toole gave his amusing sketch 'Trying a Magistrate'.
Mr Maybrick followed, gaining very loud applause for his popular
song 'The Midshipmite'. A duet for flutes by Messrs Radcliffe and
Barrett was a striking feature of this period of the evening, and
later on the first-named of these flautists gave some delightful
variations on Scotch airs. Mr E. J. Odell recited Mr H. S. Leigh's
'Legend of Furnival Inn', the performance being a fine example of the
mock-heroic style, and he was followed by Mr G. W. Anson, whose
'Men of Garlick', with its burden 'God pless der Prince of Wales'
caused uproarious laughter. Mr Arthur Mathison recited 'The
Little Hero', and Mr J. Proctor gave a clever pantomime imitation
of the business of a street juggler. Mr Pyatt then wound up the first
portion of the programme with an operatic selection.

The *Evening Standard* averred with editorial awe:

Was ever a club so honoured as the Savage? It has been entertained
in state at the Mansion House; it has returned the Lord Mayor's
hospitality. Sheriffs of London, in full pontificals, have attended its
modest banquets, and now the Prince of Wales has dined, has
smoked, has assisted with the barbarians at an evening's
amusement of the kind their soul loveth, and has become an
Honorary Member.

Edward's son, George V, subsequently became an Honorary Member,
as did *his* sons the Duke of York (later George VI), and the Duke of
Gloucester; and the present Royal incumbents of Honorary Membership
are Prince Philip and Earl Mountbatten, the Queen's uncle. Impressive as
this role of Honorary Members is, the royal linkage goes back nearly
three decades before Edward VII's election to Membership. In 1860 there
were some needy Savage widows and orphans to be looked after and
since, as usual, there was no money in the kitty it was decided to put on a
charity show for their benefit. The Lyceum Theatre was taken and a
performance of *School for Scandal* (or, possibly, scenes therefrom)

scheduled, plus a specially written burlesque version of *Ali Baba and the Forty Thieves*. There were nearly as many authors as thieves, and practically the entire Savage membership seems to have contrived its way into the cast.

What gave the performance its *cachet*, however, and enabled the price of stalls to be one guinea (normally they were one shilling) was the attendance of Queen Victoria and the Prince Consort. It seems doubtful that Her Majesty was invited (there's nothing in the Minutes about an invitation); for apart from one nobleman, the Earl of Dunraven (who was in the Club for his professional ability as the *Daily Telegraph*'s war correspondent, not for his coronet), the membership was distinctly plebian, and the notion of inviting the support of the Queen would have been thought pretentious. Evidently Her Majesty heard about the charitable object of the performance through some royal grapevine and decided to give her support. As soon as this was known the house was sold out.

A net sum of £364 was given over to the needy, and such was the success of the performance that Her Majesty let it be known that she 'would greatly approve' if the Club would take itself off up to Liverpool and play for the relief of the Lancashire Unemployed. They did, and raised £1,500 for the cause. Until the Theatre Royal was redecorated in 1908, there remained in the foyer a framed letter from the Honorary Secretary of the Aid for Distressed Unemployed Fund. It said simply: 'Old men may forget, but Lancashire never. Thank you, Savage band of gentle brothers.'

One other charitable occasion needs mentioning. When Robert Brough died in 1860 his widow and children were found to be in a distinctly parlous state, and a tremendous benefit performance was put on at Drury Lane. The advertisement for it is among the array of pictures here (page 22). 'Amateurs' meant amateur only in the sense that many Savages were appearing outside their own professions, so to speak, and self-deprecatingly insisted that, though they might be professional in their own fields, they weren't going to claim professionalism in everyone else's. The roster of 'amateurs' included Charles Dickens, Wilkie Collins, Mark Lemon (editor of *Punch*), George Cruikshank, Henry Mayhew, and Dante Rosetti – none of them exactly amateur in literature and art. Nor, according to the *Daily Telegraph*, did they do too badly on the stage:

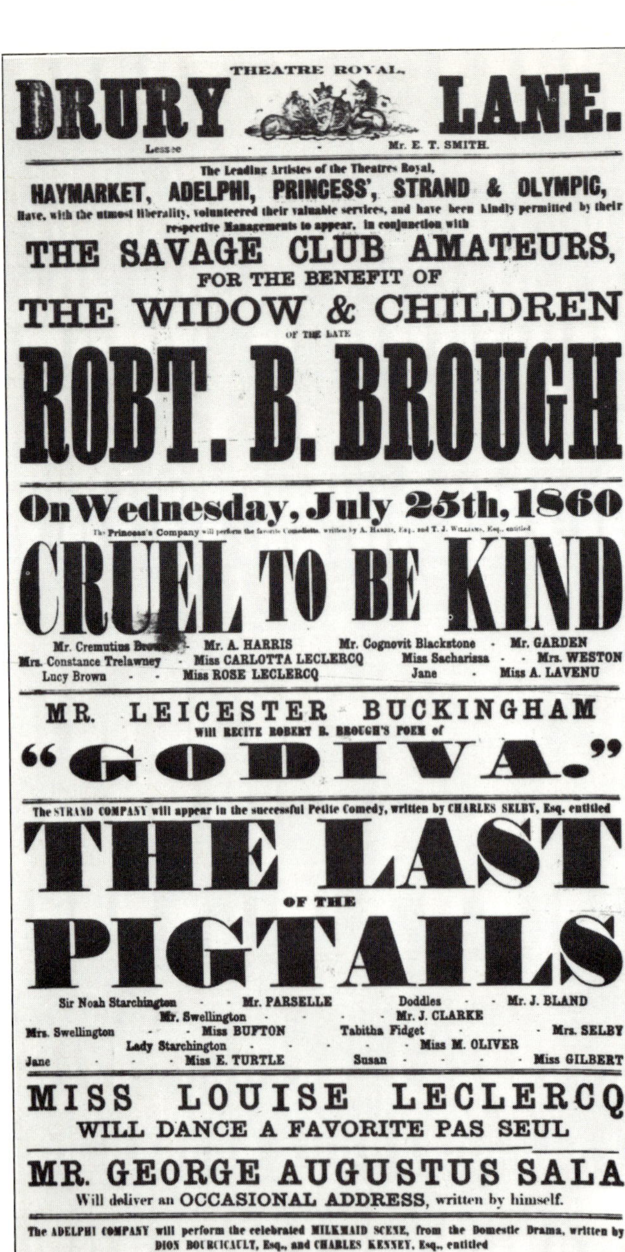

THEATRE ROYAL,
DRURY LANE.
Lessee - Mr. E. T. SMITH.
The Leading Artistes of the Theatres Royal,
HAYMARKET, ADELPHI, PRINCESS', STRAND & OLYMPIC,
Have, with the utmost liberality, volunteered their valuable services, and have been kindly permitted by their respective Managements to appear, in conjunction with
THE SAVAGE CLUB AMATEURS,
FOR THE BENEFIT OF
THE WIDOW & CHILDREN
OF THE LATE
ROBT. B. BROUGH
On Wednesday, July 25th, 1860
The Princess's Company will perform the favorite Comedietta, written by A. Harris, Esq. and T. J. Williams, Esq. entitled
CRUEL TO BE KIND
Mr. Cremutius Brown - Mr. A. HARRIS - Mr. Cognovit Blackstone - Mr. GARDEN
Mrs. Constance Trelawney - Miss CARLOTTA LECLERCQ - Miss Sacharissa - Mrs. WESTON
Lucy Brown - Miss ROSE LECLERCQ - Jane - Miss A. LAVENU
MR. LEICESTER BUCKINGHAM
WILL RECITE ROBERT B. BROUGH'S POEM of
"GODIVA."
The STRAND COMPANY will appear in the successful Petite Comedy, written by CHARLES SELBY, Esq. entitled
THE LAST
OF THE
PIGTAILS
Sir Noah Starchington - Mr. PARSELLE - Doddles - Mr. J. BLAND
Mr. Swellington - Mr. J. CLARKE
Mrs. Swellington - Miss BUFTON - Tabitha Fidget - Mrs. SELBY
Lady Starchington - Miss M. OLIVER
Jane - Miss E. TURTLE - Susan - Miss GILBERT
MISS LOUISE LECLERCQ
WILL DANCE A FAVORITE PAS SEUL
MR. GEORGE AUGUSTUS SALA
Will deliver an OCCASIONAL ADDRESS, written by himself.
The ADELPHI COMPANY will perform the celebrated MILKMAID SCENE, from the Domestic Drama, written by DION BOURCICAULT, Esq., and CHARLES KENNEY, Esq., entitled
THE WILLOW COPSE
Augustus - Mr. J. L. TOOLE - Staggers - Mr. PAUL BEDFORD
Meg - Mrs. A. MELLON (Miss Woolgar)

The late hour at which the performance terminated is our apology
for noticing the concluding piece in very brief terms. We can only
say that the members of the Savage Club fully sustained the histrionic
reputation they had acquired by their representation at the Lyceum.

With all this royal patronage going on a certain amount of lofty
reputation was bound to rub off on the Club. The Saturday Suppers
gradually became more expansive and more famous. It became something
of an honour simply to be invited to one as a guest. The *Social Register*,
a sort of *Who's Who* of the time, naturally included the name of William
Ewart Gladstone, who listed under the Honours section of his entry,
'Guest of Savage Club'. Others have felt similarly: Rachmaninoff, writing
to thank the Committee for inviting him as a guest (he subsequently
became a Member), said that only one equal honour had ever come his
way, and that was to be told that he had an English sense of humour.

It would be pointless to list the names of those who appear pictorially
in these pages; it is better to link them anecdotally with those who don't.
Pointless also to give a bleak list of the numerous homes the Club has
occupied during its 118 years. As I explained earlier, its peripatetic nature
was caused partly by the nomadic character of its members and partly
by its continual search for more suitable accommodation.

In this regard, it is, however, worth mentioning that its two longest
occupancies were at Adelphi Terrace (nearly fifty years ending in 1936),
and Carlton House Terrace (1936–1963). In both cases outside forces
made it necessary to move. Adelphi Terrace was knocked down to make
way for a dreadful Odeon-style block, and the expiring lease of the
Carlton House Terrace place (formerly Lord Curzon's home) was made
renewable at a rent ten times the amount that the Club could afford.
Variations on the 'Savages Pick Up Their Wigwams' headline have
publicized virtually every move. The most recent drollery was 'Savages
On The Move Again' in the *Evening Standard* in June 1975, when the
Club moved from St James's Street to Berkeley Square – a translation
that appears at the time of writing to be as permanent as anything can be.
It must be, unhappily, admitted at this juncture that clubs are an
anachronism today. They linger on in a world in which inflation, taxes,
regulations, rates, rents, and the difficulties of getting staff who can

MISSIONARY GLADSTONE DINES WITH THE SAVAGES.

distinguish between service and servility, render their existence theoretically impossible.

But – and this is the *raison d'être* of this book – wherever we've been, however frequently or infrequently the address on the letter paper has been changed, the House Dinners (fortnightly now, and on Fridays, instead of Saturdays, to suit the majority of Members) have gone on; and the gradually accumulating number of souvenir menus decorates the walls, wherever we are.

Matthew Norgate, who chose the selection here, frames the menus of each successive season of dinners, and a rearrangement of the entire gallery takes place to accommodate them. In the bar there stands a Tibetan wine cooler (not to shirk the obvious vapid interpolation, *I* didn't know Tibetan wines needed cooling either) to which only Matthew has the key. Into this bit of cabinetry are stuffed those menus whose time it is to give way to others. Of course they overflow even this capacious receptable (in a century and more some 2,500 have been displayed), and boxes, files, and immense albums of them pose a new storage problem each time we move. Somebody (an intrusive guest, actually) once suggested they should be got rid of as being out of keeping with the times. The Savage to whom he made this brazenly impious suggestion blanched and had to be helped to a seat and provided with a restorative glass.

Such insidious marplots aside, though, the display is a great attraction to guests. The Garrick has its Zoffanys, the Athenaeum has Faraday's invalid chair, the National Liberal has the window from which Sir Edward Grey observed that the lights were going out all over Europe; but the Savage, as one of its most ardent members, Henry Irving, pointed out, has 'the whole tapestry of its life set out upon its walls in shards of visual harmony'.

One could of course brood for years on the selection to be made; and sometimes it seems that Matthew did. Knowing him as I do, I can imagine the pulsating anguish with which he rejected so many pictures that he would have loved to see here. In a sense such a book must resemble the schoolboy's fishing net – a lot of holes joined together with string. The holes are few and the string thin because the book can be only as thick as you see it.

Be assured, though, that, even if far from complete, the selection is truly representative. The Club itself, the Royals, the famous guests, the writers, musicians, artists, scientists and lawyers, the loved entertainers, even the card players – they all get a fair showing. The commentary that accompanies them is intended not as a distraction – the pictures deserve your full attention, many of them for the brilliance of their drawing or the wit behind their ideas – but as enlightenment where such seems necessary, and to give a complementary verbal picture of the Club's character.

Not So Savage

TAKE THE MUSICIANS. 'And take them as far away as possible' was the usual comment of Bert Thomas, famous in his time for his comic drawings in *Punch*, and specially famous for his World War I drawing of the insouciant Tommy pausing to light his pipe while he murmurs, ' 'Arf a mo', Kaiser'. Bert was intolerant of practically everything and everybody. Shakespeare's words, Elgar's music, and the drawings of Leonardo and Phil May were acceptable; so were a few Savages. All the rest was dross beneath his contempt, even though his contempt was freely voiced. Bert occasionally expressed his contempt too freely for his fellows; one day in the washroom when in the presence of B. C. Hilliam (the Flotsam bit of the 'Flotsam and Jetsam' duo), he spoke slightingly of one of Hilliam's friends and was upended into the basket full of soiled towels with the comment: 'If you want to wash dirty linen in public you'd better join it.'

As I was saying when Bertie so rudely interrupted me, take the musicians. Indeed, combine the two by taking Bertie's depiction of Landon Ronald (page 28) – a brilliant caricature in which the edge of malice is blunted by the wit of the conception. A similar wit conveys the impassivity of Moiseiwitsch's features, whether he was playing poker or the piano (page 30).

There are more Club stories about Benno and his excitable sibling pianist Mark Hambourg (page 32) than about any other Savages. One of

the most famous happened thus: Benno entered the card-room one day
to find Mark (whose range of tone included an exceptionally loud
fortissimo) absent from the poker table. He enquired about Mark's
whereabouts and was told he was playing in Newcastle. 'Really?' said
Benno, cupping his hand to his ear, 'I can't hear him.'

Another celebrated story concerns the occasion when the excitable
Mark came charging into the Club, encountered Benno and pitchforked
out his news.

'Benno, Benno, they are to make a film of the life of Beethoven and
I am to play Beethoven!'

'So!' Moiseiwitsch replied in his slow guttural speech. 'And who is to
play the piano?'

For good measure I'll edge in with a personal Benno anecdote. He gave
his first provincial recital in Reading, where I live, and fifty years later
came back and repeated the programme, the magnificent centre-piece of
which was the set of four Ballades by Chopin. I reported this jubilee
performance for the local paper, but, as is the way with local papers,
'ballades' got misprinted as 'bollades'. When eventually the report filtered
through to Benno via his press cutting agency, he sent me a postcard
inscribed in his spidery handwriting: 'And Bollades to you too'.

Sidney Strube, who was as famous for his 'Little Man' as was David
Low for 'Colonel Blimp', and who called everyone George regardless of
age or sex, has, so to speak, en-staved the rotund Welsh tenor Parry Jones,
page 34; and on page 36, Low himself shows off another rotundity,
Lord Hewart, the Lord Chief Justice, who announced that Benno would
play by saying dramatically, 'It is my duty to sentence Brother Savage
Benno Moiseiwitsch to fifteen minutes' hard labour, during which he will
execute Wagner and Liszt. The remainder of the Brother Savages I bind
over, jointly and severally, to keep the peace for that period.'

Many members of the famous London orchestras have been, and are,
Savages. Two of the three generations of flautist Walkers are happily still
with us (page 38), and Alan Civil (page 40), principal horn of the
BBC Symphony Orchestra, frequently compounds the most extraordinary
combinations of instruments in his blazing finales to the entertainments.
Whatever the combination, the ensemble is always known as the
Philsavonia, a name I'm pleased to admit I bestowed – my sole

SAVAGE
CLUB
HOUSE
DINNER
APRIL 30TH 1921.
"DOWN IN THE FOREST"
Landon
Ronald
in the
Chair

contribution to the musical life of the Club, apart from an occasional quavering solo spot in the choruses with which the entertainment part of the evening always begins. Herman Finck – another essay in rotundity – looking remarkably like Arnold Bennett, had the Paul Whiteman band (page 42); but we cherish the Philsavonia, which at the last count, at Sydney Tafler's dinner (page 44), numbered fifteen, including the euphonium in the bell of which the Club cat was found sleeping next morning.

(There is, incidentally, a certain dotty logic in the sequence of pictures here displayed. It may baffle you, and it will certainly have you skipping about a bit – as William Murdoch, the Australian pianist (page 46), is poised to do in his kangaroo suit – but who are you not to be baffled?)

Annual Dinners. Hardly surprisingly, there's one each year to celebrate the founding of the Club, each with a notable guest of honour. The drawings for them are scattered through the book and not many of them demand any explanation. Exceptionally, perhaps, I should mention that the being peering over Osbert Lancaster's shoulder (page 48) is not me but Maudie Littlehampton, Sir Osbert's creation. I'm the one in the postage-stamp drawing with the convict eyebrows and the hair, apparently about to fall over backwards. Not specially relevant but worth mentioning is that the physician Lord Horder, who was Chaired by Tedder (page 50), was the subject of a clerihew written by the present incumbent of the Horder lordship, my first publisher:

> Lord Dawson of Penn
> Has killed many many men
> But not so many as Lord Horder
> Who kills them to order.

Neither of their lordships was a Savage, but we've had a rich sprinkling from the peerage as you will see. True, you can't see much of Baldwin (page 52), but the object of the drawing is to display the magnificence of the staircase at Carlton House Terrace, the right wall of which was covered by an immense mural by the Harker Brothers (who appear on pages 54 and 56). The carpet up which the Earl is sweeping had recently been presented by him to the Club. The top of the staircase and the landing between the drawing-room and dining-room can be seen in the

Allegretto tranquillo

Andante espressivo

Allegretto di molto

Adagio non troppo

Molto allegro vivace

Allegro con fuoco

Poco agitato

Presto agitato

Agitato e con fuoco

SAVAGE CLUB HOUSE DINNER · 21ˢᵗ OCT. 1933
Benno Moiseiwitsch in the Chair.

drawing in which Alan Brock is lighting fireworks (page 58). Being king-pin of the famous firework firm of that name, he was never let off the Guy Fawkes Night celebrations. However, he was justly more proud of being an amateur criminologist and fingerprint expert, and of writing expertly and entertainingly on those subjects. Another obvious candidate for the Chair on those explosive November nights was Guy Bousfield; but why he appeared adorned with fireworks on 11 April 1953 (page 60) is a Club puzzle to which I can offer no solution other than a paucity of ideas in the artist that week.

The versatility of invention in House Dinner menu cards is, in general, remarkable. You don't need to know anything about Fred Gorle to be able to add him up from the figures on pages 62 and 64; or about Raven Hill's gourmandizing tendencies from his self-portrait on page 65 and Bertie Thomas's on page 66. On the subject of food I can quote Somerset Maugham, who, though not pictured here, had been a guest at the dinner given for Marconi in 1903 (page 63) and was a guest in 1960. He recalled that at the Marconi dinner the menu ran to soups, patés, fish, three entrées, four puddings, ices, two savouries, cheese and celery, and coffee. The cost: three shillings and sixpence.

He reminisced further: 'Although I had just finished walking the wards of St Thomas's hospital and had a certain familiarity with medicine, I was unable to cure the indigestion that resulted from the dinner. But I was cured by the Savage Club barman, who mixed me a concoction so fiery that it would have cured a corpse of its affliction.'

On the subject of club servants, I must point out that they are a special breed (as the first of the Gorle cards indicates) – very rare and becoming rarer. Savage servants, though, are rarer than that: they are unique. They are perfectly capable of saying on the phone, with the utmost conviction, 'Madam, there are *no* husbands in the Club.' But then all other clubs' major domos have said the same thing countless times. It takes a Savage head porter, however, to arrange for his wife to telephone the Honorary Secretary's office to say: 'Hudson presents his compliments, Sir, but regrets he will be unable to take duty at the Club today as, unfortunately, he passed away during the night.'

And on the subject of the eagle-eyed – which I wasn't, but am willing to digress – let me choke the chortles of those who have spotted the

59th
SAVAGE CLUB
House Dinner
In the Chair
Mark Hambourg
Saturday Oct 19th 1917

32

name of Charles Dickens as proposing the toast to the guest of honour at the breakfast given to the American actors in London in 1880 (page 67). I *know* the novelist died in 1870. This was his eldest son; and the toast he was proposing was to the United States Ambassador (as we should now call him), James Russell Lowell, Longfellow's successor in the Chair of Modern Languages at Harvard, the first Editor of *The Atlantic Monthly*, and a poet in his own right (most famous for *The Biglow Papers*). Lowell had made some slightly acid remarks about the English character in an essay called 'A Certain Condescension in Foreigners', and, since there were a lot of American actors in London at the time, it was thought to be a bright idea to assemble them together and honour them together with their Ambassador (at breakfast, of course, because they were working men in the evenings). Apparently the occasion was a great success, diplomatically as well as entertainingly. *The World* said approvingly:

> If ever an excellent speaker had an appreciative audience, the American Minister certainly enjoyed that advantage at the entertainment given by the Savage Club to the American actors. The speech was admirable in itself, perfectly delivered, in a soft, low-toned, yet penetrating voice, and every point was taken instantly and applauded to the echo. Rarely have orator and audience been so well attuned.

The Club and the American nation had been well attuned quite a while before that occasion. Mark Twain (page 68) had been elected in the previous decade – it was at a House Dinner that he made his much quoted remark about Chaucer and Spenser and Shakespeare and Milton being dead, 'and I'm not feeling very well myself'. Stephen Fiske, Augustin Daly, W. J. Florence, William John McCullough – all famous in theatre and literature in their time – were Savages too. In more recent times we've had James Dyrenforth (page 69), the actor and lyricist who wrote the words of 'Garden in the Rain' – Carrol Gibbons wrote the music. He never relinquished his American passport but lived in, and loved, England for almost fifty years, calling himself 'England's oldest living metic'. Even now his Chicago accent still seems to echo round the place; recently Basil Boothroyd (Prince Philip's biographer) plucked it out

SAVAGE CLUB
HOUSE DINNER
PARRY JONES IN THE CHAIR!
JAN 22 1955
STRUBE
THE MASTERSINGER, LOOK YOU!

of the air when he recalled that Jimmy, on hearing a guest referring somewhat pedantically to a one-legged man as a uniped, remarked that it sounded like a cure for unicorns. Ironically, Jimmy died after a thrombosis and the consequent amputation of one of his legs.

That concludes, more or less, the tour of the American peaks; but leaves one Russian peak – apart from Rachmaninoff (page 70), Moiseiwitsch, and Hambourg – unmentioned. Ivan Maisky (page 71), Russia's Ambassador to the Court of St James's during World War II, cherished his Honorary Savage Membership so much that after his return to the Kremlin he set up a long-lingering correspondence with the most improbable of correspondents, George Wood (page 72), doyen of the music-hall he inhabited as long as it was there to inhabit, and known throughout those many decades as Wee Georgie Wood. (He reverted to plain George along with the dignified award of an O.B.E.)

The Wood drawing is one of a great many in the Club – and in this book – by John Worsley. Neither the signature nor the style is difficult to to spot. John Worsley became famous just after the war, but at that time less for his paintings, drawings, and sculpture than for the 'Albert, R.N.' exploit in which he contrived and manufactured a dummy to cover the escape of a prisoner from his German P.O.W. camp. Turned into narrative, the exploit became a popular film, play, and radio drama during the 1950s. Today, though, the Worsley reputation justly rests on his versatility as a portrait painter, marine artist, book illustrator, and visual interpreter of stories for children on television; his *Wind in the Willows*, *Treasure Island*, and *Christmas Carol* found an enormous audience. His ability to capture a likeness in benevolent caricature means that he is much called upon by Savages trembling with apprehension at the thought of their forthcoming House Dinner Chairmanship. Harry Riley (page 73), whom he succeeded as the most prolific of the menu card artists, was similarly beset, as the number of drawings bearing *his* signature will testify.

Three paragraphs back, I muttered the name of Basil Boothroyd without mentioning more than that he is Prince Philip's biographer – which indeed he is. However, he is more important to me here (or, rather, on page 74, where he may be seen gleefully and enviably chairing Miss Katherine Whitehorn on his knee) as introducing the tricky subject of

SAVAGE CLUB
HOUSE DINNER
FELLOW SAVAGES
CONSIDER
YOUR VERDICT
SATURDAY 12TH OCTOBER 1935.
BARON HEWART OF BURY
IN THE CHAIR.

L A D I E S. Despite the sentiments of one testy old Savage – 'I love 'em all, but not in my Club' – *tempora* and *mores* ever whizz by. Nowadays we let the girls decorate the drawing-room after 5.30 in the evenings. Their Savage husbands or swain may there ply them with drinks and entertain them while they long to edge nearer to the forbidden bar and confirm their secret opinion that the laughter they hear is rooted in ribaldry. It rarely is, but there's no convincing them of that.

The proper Ladies' Night, of which several respesentative menu drawings appear here, is, however, a very firmly founded institution in the Savage Club – or, rather, out of it; for until the end of the 1960s it was always held in a suitable hotel. This was instituted after a disastrous decision in 1891 to admit women to certain selected House Dinners. No one had imagined that the fascinations of the Club would compel them to impose their presence long after their husbands were ready to depart; but such was the case, and House Dinners with ladies were peremptorily abandoned in a Minute by the Honorary Secretary, Sir Somers Vine, to the effect that 'Ladies' Nights within the Club would prove its ruination.' A certain gallantry prevailed, however, and an annual Ladies' Savage Club Banquet was settled for. It was usually held at the Hotel Cecil, newly built and, with 1,000 rooms, the biggest hotel in the world. When the Cecil was demolished in 1930 to make way for Shell-Mex House, the venue for Ladies' Nights was changed to the Park Lane Hotel. Nowadays we're fortunate enough to have access to a dining-room that is big enough to accommodate a well-attended Ladies' Night.

As if this annual spree (the only Club function, incidentally, at which Savages wear evening dress) were not enough, we also have an annual cocktail party and the occasional, aptly named, Distaff Diversion, in which an informal after-dinner entertainment is given – usually in the form of a talk or recital – with the 'Distaff' happily frequenting the bar without let or hindrance throughout the evening. Nobody can say we don't pay due observance to femininity.

Still on the subject of ladies and their nights, you will note that the card for that of 1953 (page 75) was drawn by that remarkably fine Savage artist Robert Sherriffs. He also did the caricatures of 'Mr H.' – Leslie Henson – (page 76), Tommy Handley (page 77), and Alan

Savage Club House Dinner
In the Chair
Brother Savage
GORDON WALKER
APRIL 28th 1962
Fillet of Sole Mornay
Tournedos Provençale
Buttered Peas
New Potatoes
Canapé Savage
Coffee
Harry Riley

Herbert and Compton Mackenzie (page 78). All of them exemplify the
firm clarity of his line, his uncanny ability to capture a likeness, and the
perfect balance of his composition. He died, alas, too young; during his
Savage Membership he contributed not only impeccable drawings but
also an astonishing amount of erudition on, seemingly, any subject that
came up for discussion in the bar. Heraldry (on which he was an
acknowledged expert), music ('Bach! That bloody bell-ringer!'), literature
(he could easily quote, if the occasion warranted it, from an immense
range of prose and verse), folklore, horticulture – there were few subjects
that left him without an informative word to say. His lean, rangy figure
and triangular feline face, chokered at the neck with a silk cravat,
sometimes populated the Club for days and nights on end; then, as
suddenly, he would disappear and not be seen for months. I once asked
him, just before he vanished, whether he would consider drawing a
likeness of me for a personal Christmas card. He evidently brooded over
my possibilities while he was away; and as it turned out that I was
standing in the bar when next he entered the Club, he came straight up
to me, as if there had been no break in the conversation, and said
regretfully that he feared there was 'nothing to draw'.

His drawing of Tommy Handley, of course, cannot be passed without
some mention of ITMA. Most of the illustrious ITMA team were
Savages: Jack Train (page 79), Fred Yule, Clarence Wright, Ted
Kavanagh and Tommy himself. The 'ITMA table' in the dining-room
was where most of the scripts were put together at lunchtime on the day
of the broadcast. Much of the content of *Punch*, in the days when it was
funny, was also conceived in the Savage bar and dining-room. The
Editor, Bernard Hollowood, and Art Editor, Russell Brockbank, were
invariably joined at the lunchtime session by some of the *Punch* team of
writers and artists – be it Richard Mallett, Richard Price, Basil Boothroyd,
Alex Atkinson, Norman Thelwell, John Taylor, André François, Michael
ffolkes or the Australian George Sprod (whose menu on page 80 is
drawn by ffolkes). Nowadays the magazine is fuller of advertising than
of wit, which, in the changing nature of things, is probably good for the
proprietors, if not for the readers – more *tempora*, more *mores*.

In the matter of change, nothing is more evident in this book than the
difference, spread over more than a century, in drawing techniques and

SAVAGE CLUB HOUSE DINNER
APRIL 17 1970
at 86 St. James's Street, S.W. 1
The music goes roun' an' aroun', and it comes out here!
"and here!"
"and here!"
in the chair
ALAN CIVIL
MENU
Lentil Soup
Roast Sirloin of Beef
Yorkshire Pudding
Roast Potatoes
Sprouts
Cheddar or Cheshire Cheese
Coffee
"and here!"
"and here!"
"and here!"
John Worsley

presentation. Compare, for example, Harry Furniss's card for the first
Royal dinner (page 81) with Tom Webster's for the Duke of York,
later George VI, (page 82); or the crowded Victorian drawing-room
effect in Bernard Gribble's celebration of Admiral Jellicoe's election
(page 83) with the sparse lines of Bert Thomas's Starr Wood (page 84).
There is, of course, nothing wrong with any of these styles. They simply
reflect what is acceptable to the audience of a particular age, though
sometimes they are oddly prophetic. In 1886, for instance, two complaints
were lodged about the 'bareness' of Dudley Hardy's drawing (page 85).
His uncluttered style turned out to anticipate the spacious design that,
by the 1920s, was not only acceptable but admirable. Aubrey Hammond's
drawing for the actor Leon M. Lion (page 86) was topical too, as his
apologies to the symbol of the British Empire Exhibition signify.

To return to the Harry Furniss card: in the middle, camera right of
H.R.H. and left of the Messrs Radcliffe and Barrett and their flutes, is
visible a histrionic figure whose neck, apparently, has been caught in a
draught, declaiming 'The Legend of Furnival Inn'. That was – perhaps I
should say *is*, his legend lingers yet – Edwin Jehoshophat Odell, whom I
mentioned in the Introduction as living, like Richard Savage, the Club's
Godfather, on the charity of his friends.

This, God knows, E. J. Odell did. All that seems to be established
about his professional career is that he was an actor with the Henry
Irving company and specialized in Shakespeare's clowns. Aaron Watson,
who established that much, also says of him:

As an entertainer, and peculiarly as an entertainer at the Club, where
he is always sublimely at his ease, Mr Odell has a most remarkable
individuality. He plays up to himself, as it were. He has a pretty
wit, of a kind more common in the Bohemia of an earlier day, and
his playful introductions to his songs or recitations are often the
best part of the fun. His repertoire is as extensive as are his means
of expressing the various emotions, and many of his pieces have been
written expressly for himself. These, I believe, he proposes to publish,
with illustrations by artists who are members of the Savage Club.
For a while Mr Odell ceased to appear on the Saturday nights, and
he was, of course, very much missed. He is one of types that there
is no replacing.

SAVAGE CLUB
HOUSE DINNER
APRIL 7th 1923
HERMAN FINCK
IN THE CHAIR
SUPPORTED BY
PAUL WHITEMAN & HIS BAND

Aaron Watson was, of course, the Club's historian and was writing when Odell was still alive. That, no doubt, explains his tactful omission of the reason for Odell's absence – it was one of the many times he was suspended or expelled from the Club. He was a dreadful old scoundrel who was carpeted before the Committee so many times – usually for failing to pay his dues or his bar bills or both, or for unwarrantably insulting some distinguished guest – that he might have been beating a path to the residence of the inventor of the better mousetrap. He was egotistical, rude, possessive, mean and grasping. But he was (very much in quotes) a 'character', and, however many times he was pushed out of the Club and the porters forbidden to let him in again, he always came back – patriarchal, wide-awake, be-hatted – and resumed his seat in what he called 'my' chair. 'Here Old Odell sat' reads a brass plate on that very chair; and sit he did, forever scrounging drinks and smokes ('I will have a large Irish whiskey and a cigar'), insulting contemporaries and squashing new Members – particularly those who tried to tell stories in the bar, which they sometimes mistakenly did. No one could give them their come-uppance more effectively than Odell. Having sneered at frequent intervals through a narrative painfully undertaken and as painfully ended, he would say contemptuously, 'Young man, there's a *humorous* version of that tale.'

In his own opinion, Odell's long membership – expulsions and suspensions apart, he was elected in 1873 and died in a charitable institution, Charterhouse, in 1928, Savagely supported to the end with food, drink, and tobacco – entitled him to the privilege of insulting everybody, including top people. When the Duke of York was invited to a House Dinner as a guest and, unknowingly, sat in Odell's chair, the old man fumed at him: 'How dare you, sir! That's *my* chair!' H.R.H. hastily apologized and took himself off to the bar.

No one really knew Odell's age. He was continually being given seventieth, eightieth, and ninetieth birthday dinners. If the menu card on page 87 is right and his eightieth birthday was in 1894, he must have been 114 when he died, which seems improbably ancient. However statistically unsatisfactory, his simultaneous septua-, octo-, and nonagenarianism was a carefully fostered Club joke. In 1904 the same menu card was dished up again with the substitution of 'Odell's *1904th*

SAVAGE CLUB HOUSE DINNER
FOLLIES
LAST PERFORMANCE AT THIS THEATRE
at 86 St. James's
St. SW1
2nd May 1975
IN THE CHAIR
STAR OF STAGE FILM TELEVISION
CARD ROOM AND RACECOURSE
BROTHER SAVAGE
SYDNEY TAFLER
WITH A SUPPORTING BILL
featuring
VEGETABLE SOUP
CAUCASIAN LAMB CUTLETS
NEW POTATOES
PEAS
CHEESE
COFFEE

Birthday'. Whatever his age, many Savages saw him – and still see him
– as an exemplar of the Club's spirit of individuality, irreverence, and
independence. (Though how he could have claimed the last with all that
parasitical drinking is beyond comprehension.) He seems to me, on all
the evidence, to have been an unmitigated old bounder.

Bounder or not, he is, as I say, immortalized in Savage history –
orally in the true and apocryphal tales that are told of him, and
marmoreally in the marble bust displayed in the bar. That piece of
sculpture was the work of Albert Toft, eminent (*eminent? What am I
saying? Of course he was eminent or he wouldn't have been in the Club!*)
– eminent for his portrait busts and his war memorials, which are to be
seen in many midland and northern cities. Toft exhibited his work
continuously for forty-one years at the Royal Academy and is to be seen
committing one of his idealized monoliths, while he waits for the bar to
open, in the House Dinner card on page 88. He is on view again on page
89, dressed, as was his custom, in an Edwardianly waisted suit, spats, and
flowing bow tie and in the act of immortalizing the diminutive Charley
Hands. Charles, who beamed and bounced about the Club like a latex
cherub, was improbably, but truly, among the toughest and most famous
of World War I war correspondents. He is also famous for saying to a
visiting harpsichordist who had played at a House Dinner – and saying
it with a beaming smile – 'Charming! Charming! Like the wires of a
birdcage plucked with a fork!'

Of the two artists who executed these drawings, George Stampa and
'Poy', more in a moment; meanwhile a word about the distinguished
gentleman in the distinguished chair on page 90. James Agate, theatre
critic, wit, man about town, and splendid Savage, wrote constantly about
the Club in his *Ego* series of autobiographical volumes, and in *Ego 8*
quotes his friend, the actor Cedric Hardwicke, an equally Savage Savage:

Cedric was in immense form and full of stories. How a famous
Hollywood star, who poses as a great art connoisseur, bought a
vastly expensive fake Manet or Renoir – Cedric couldn't remember
which. Only to find, when he got home, the original hanging on his
walls! . . . He was full of theories about himself. 'I can't act. I have
never acted. And I shall never act. What I can do is suspend my

SAVAGE CLUB
HOUSE DINNER
MARCH 26
1927
1
William Murdoch
IN THE CHAIR

audience's power of judgement till I've finished . . .' [Apropos] *Hamlet*
he said he thought the best King there had ever been was Oscar Asche:
'When he looked at Gertrude the corners of his lower lip hung down
like mutton chops.' He said that never before or since had the
atmosphere of the court of Denmark been properly conveyed. 'It
should be gross and licentious. Nowadays the place is so prim and
Claudius so proper that you wonder what all the fuss is about.'

A range of Agate's caustic *mots* are still much quoted (and sometimes
stolen), nearly thirty years after his death. A couple of them can be slipped
in here without burning holes in the paper. At Adelphi Terrace, the Club
had a little librarian named Willie Richardson who was always scratching
away with a squeaky pen on scraps of paper – 'a sound', Agate said,
'like mice copulating in a wastepaper basket'. On entering the grand new
premises in Carlton House Terrace, he said he felt 'like a debutante with
a hole in her stocking'.

The Savage in full feathered fig on page 91, Max Pemberton, wears
no stockings to be thus deficient, but the insignia of his novels handsomely
decorate his head. He and Rafael Sabatini, in equally full fig on page 92
and apparently bothered about his temperature, were the match, in their
day, of the authors of such excitements as *Z Cars* and *Crossroads* (who,
incidentally, are among today's Members). True, the readers of their
books might be numbered in thousands rather than the television's
millions, but their names were, as the cliché has it, on everyone's lips.
Pemberton, who had been editor of *Chums* and *Cassell's Magazine* and
had founded the London School of Journalism, wrote exciting novels of
the sea. These were of the kind in which *aficionados* of the late Douglas
Fairbanks delighted when they were filmed – *The Iron Pirate*, *Sea Wolves*,
Captain Black. Sabatini also embraced the swashbuckling genre in
The Sea Hawk, *Captain Blood*, and *Scaramouche*. Like their Brother
Savages Michael Arlen and Edgar Wallace (page 93 – but that's one of
his readers, not him), who were famous in different genres of literature,
they were recognized, like Beatles or Rolling Stones, everywhere they
went. However, their visits to the Club were always an escape from
adulation, not a search for it.

This observation provides an excuse for quoting one of the most

The 112th Savage Club Annual Dinner
Nov 13th 1970
In the Chair
Brother Savage
ALAN WYKES
Guest of Honour
OSBERT LANCASTER
C.B.E.
Menu
Tomato Soup
Steak, Kidney & Mushroom Pudding
Brussels Sprouts
Mashed Potatoes
Cheddar or Cheshire Cheese
Coffee
ffolkes

characteristic remarks ever made in the Club – one that distills the very
quintessence of its spirit. Percy Bradshaw (of whom, with Stampa and
'Poy', more in a moment), wrote of his earliest days in the Club:

> I had been to the Savage as a guest two or three times, but when I
> first entered the old Club in the Adelphi to do my 'month's probation'
> I felt very like a new boy at a public school. I was soon put at my
> ease by a group of members in the north-west room [the bar]. They
> were men at whom I had often gazed in awe – Mark Hambourg
> and Moiseiwitsch, George Stampa and George Belcher, A. P. Herbert,
> Rafael Sabatini, Max Pemberton, and Norman O'Neill. I was
> astonished at the friendliness of all the august strangers. I saw no
> realization by any of them that they were important people. They
> suggested a crowd of happy schoolboys. I mentioned my surprise
> to Bart Kennedy [page 94], to whom I was introduced. 'You'll soon
> get used to it, my boy', he smiled. 'Savages always hang their haloes
> in the hall.'

And woe betide you if you don't. One new Savage, whose name I shall
allow to be mercifully washed away by the tides of iniquity, once
embarked on a recital of his achievements. He was no more than a few
feet from the shore when he was squelched with the comment: 'You're
giving yourself a hell of a welcome, aren't you?'

Percy V. Bradshaw (the V's designation was a secret between him and
himself) was a marvellously successful illustrator who ran a marvellously
successful correspondence course in art – ironically commented on by
Strube on page 95. He was an extremely gentle soul much given to
exquisite courtesies, and wore his dark hair in a cowlick over his forehead;
both of which characteristics obviously gave Tom Purvis the idea for the
second Bradshaw menu card on page 96. The idea of Percy as a dictator
was so ludicrous – in any case, Hitler was, in 1935, a comic, rather than a
sinister, figure – and the purloining of Club joke V to turn him into a
von so apposite, that for years the drawing was given a place of isolated
distinction on the bar walls. Gradually, however, it became more and
more difficult to explain its subtleties to visitors, who tended to imagine
the Club was harbouring the London branch of the Nazi Party.

Now, if you've been able to bear your soul in patience for news of

Savage Club.
96th Annual Dinner.
Guest of the Club - LORD HORDER.
Brother Savage
LORD TEDDER
in the CHAIR
who, quite
rightly.
Crashes
through
the
Savage
Club
Choir's
December
5th
1953.
SOUND BARRIER.

'Poy' (page 97) and G. L. Stampa (page 98), I have news for you.
'Poy' was the signature of Percy Fearon, who, having been raised in New
Jersey, where Jersey was Joisey, uttered his own name likewise, and made
it Poisy. This, naturally and quickly, became abbreviated to Poy. As for
his career – Lord Northcliffe hired him as cartoonist to the *Daily Mail*;
but at the time the other horse in that stable, the *Evening News*, was
losing the field and Northcliffe got Poy to draw the cartoon for the
News's 10,000th number. The contents bill announced 'Poy's first picture'
(Northcliffe didn't understand the word cartoon), and the *News* thereupon
raised a gallop and was duly saved from the knacker's yard. Enter thus,
into the hall of fame, Poy and his perceptive glances into the mind of
John Citizen who, like Strube's 'Little Man', for years spoke up and
waved umbrellas for the man on the Clapham omnibus.

George Loraine Stampa exhibited portraits at the Royal Academy,
but it was by his innumerable drawings for *Punch* (especially those
connected with the theatre) that he was best known. He was not in
essence a comic artist, in the sense that he made visual jokes, but, rather,
a witty barer of people's characters in beautifully drawn likenesses.
Besides those I've mentioned, there are several other examples of
Stampa's and Poy's work in this book. Looking for them makes for
good critical exercise. Both the Fearons and the Stampas are represented,
I'm delighted to be able to say, in the Club today – the Fearons by Henry,
for many years 'Fieldfare' of the *Evening News*, and the Stampas by
Arthur, happily retired from the film world.

The beautiful architectural drawing by Donald Blake on page 99
needs some explanation. It gives the impression that the Club house at
1 Carlton House Terrace is falling apart. Actually it was pushed apart
by a Luftwaffe bomb on 15 October 1940, and the drawing shows the
final work of restoration going on (eight years later, you will note).
Partial restoration was accomplished in time for the Annual Dinner to
be held on 7 December 1940, when, with James Agate in the Chair,
Hugh Ross Williamson contributed, as part of the entertainment, a
personal reminiscence of the bombing by Reginald Pound (page 100).
Pound was the biographer of, *inter alios*, Northcliffe, Henry Wood,
Alfred Munnings, Gordon Selfridge, and Prince Albert; not to mention
the *Strand Magazine*, of which he was a sometime editor. He wrote this:

SAVAGE CLUB
HOUSE DINNER
In the Chair
The EARL BALDWIN
of BEWDLEY
Saturday March 6th 1954
1 Carlton House Terrace · S·W·1

52

There is an Eastern saying which you probably know: 'learn to distinguish between incidents and events.' The bomb coming down on the Club yesterday morning seemed like an event to me, and it has not yet receded to the proportions of an incident. No doubt it will.

It arrived with the roar of an express train twelve feet from where I was lying in the nursery of the steward's flat down below. The more egotistic one is, the more one tends, naturally, to dramatize these personal happenings in wartime, but it does appear that I had a fairly lucky escape. I won't bore you with the details, except to say that a search party was sent down to find me, failed, and reported me missing. Also this: a lump of Regency stonework weighing a good two hundredweight landed on my pillow. It couldn't have missed me by more than a couple of inches. Spiked iron railings from somewhere outside were forced into the room, what remained of it, and that could have been nasty too. The fear of gas escaping from the mains was for me the worst experience of all; it really was frightening. I suppose now that it was the smell of the bomb.

The ceiling had come down on me, and I couldn't get out for some minutes because the door was jammed. I had to crawl under it. The passage outside had collapsed like a tent. The steward's sitting-room was smashed up, but I saw in the half-light that two eggs that had been put on the mantelpiece overnight were still there, intact. When at last I got out onto the stone stairs, I nearly fainted with relief at finding that I wasn't going to die, that I was wet with perspiration and not with blood, as I had thought. I had only one sock on and no shoes, and yet, picking my way through shoals of broken glass, I did not get a scratch.

Groping my way upstairs I noticed, for the first time, the strange deathly silence of the place. There didn't seem to be a sign of life left in the Club. It was extraordinary. I wondered what I was going to find when I got up into the hall.

I found someone huddled against the wall leading to what, a few minutes before, had been the library. A very odd figure in the dimness and the dust; it might have been Dr Pangloss waiting to explain to me the necessity of bombs in the best of all possible

SAVAGE CLUB
HOUSE DINNER
APRIL 25 1925
R. HARKER
THE SONS OF THE HARKER
IN THE CHAIR

worlds. I then saw that it was Brother Savage Tom Clare sobbing
his heart out. He was in a frightful mess. His face was a grotesque
mask of plaster and blood, his eyes huge red saucers, like a clown's,
spilling tears. I helped him to shuffle along to the ladies' lounge.
As he sat there in his golf suit, with the brilliantly diced stockings,
complete with funny little tabs, his monocle a crimson disc on his
pullover, he did indeed look a sorry human sight.

But he very soon pulled himself together, and gallantly protested
to the first-aid people that there were others who needed help more
than he. Then a pretty little ambulance girl, who looked as if she
had come straight from a beauty parlour – she had make-up on her
face and a neat little triangle of handkerchief sticking out of her
top pocket – coaxed him onto a stretcher, and Tom was carried off,
waving us goodbye as he went.

Then a fire started next door. Then a fire at the ex-German
Embassy along the Terrace. Then a fire at the Union Club. Then a
fire at the Carlton Club. Then a fire at the Reform . . . All around
us the sky was plumed and pennanted with fire . . . Toward seven in
the morning, exhaustion began to come upon us. It had been a long
night of emergency and tension and strain, nearly twelve hours
of it. . . .

I remember, and I hope I shall always remember, the goodness
of everybody involved in the affair, welded by a sense of catastrophe
into a unity of selflessness that seems to me to have been a fine and
heartening thing. There was a touch of splendour about, the
splendour of men living up to the very best that is in them. It was
exhilarating.

That reminiscence having been read and having made its immensely
poignant impact, it was the turn of Leslie Henson to entertain the
assembled company; but he refused, saying simply, 'You can't follow
that.'

To return to less momentous things, the chalk drawing on page 101
is of Dylan Thomas (who was a Savage) by Mervyn Levy (who *is* a
Savage). It is worth noting, I think, that Dylan's financial shenanigans

SAVAGE CLUB DEC 20th 19

Joseph Harker

IN THE CHAIR

ROLAND HARKER
DEC. 1919

56

were taken care of by the Committee, who gave instructions that the Club
was to continue accepting his cheques even though they were so rarely
honoured that it was found to be worth 'minuting' when one had been.
The similarly un-captioned picture on page 102 is a self-portrait by
Joseph Simpson, a distinguished member of the Royal Society of British
Artists as well as of the Savage, whose quality as an artist can be assessed
by the candour of his sartorial revelation. The wacky-looking dog
bulging benevolently out of the chair in the drawing on page 103 is
Bonzo, a strip- and postcard-character as famous in his day as Charlie
Brown is today and Felix, Popeye, and Pip, Squeak and Wilfred were
then. He was the creation of the signatory of the card, George Studdy.

In the matter of creations, none could be more marvellous, or more
affectionately regarded, than those of Heath Robinson, whose contrivance
for splitting the atom (page 104) celebrated the visit of Sir James Jeans
in 1938. His son Oliver, an artist in his own right and for many years
Editor of *Good Housekeeping*, was recently elevated by general
acclamation (as was John Worsley) to the lofty status of Trustee of the
Club. There are four of these, the other two being Macdonald Hastings
and Reginald Pound, and they seem to be severally and collectively
responsible, legally, for the Club and its ship of property and all who sail
in her. Thus loftily pinnacled, Oliver continues conscientiously to attend
all Committee meetings.

One artist mentioned in passing deserves a few more words. Phil May,
a Yorkshireman born in 1864, died at the age of thirty-nine. But from
1878, when he started as an assistant scene painter at the Grand Theatre,
Leeds, his fame slowly spread, mostly through the medium of *Punch*
where he succeeded to the place formerly held by George du Maurier.
A stint of work in Australia, where only primitive printing techniques
were available, compelled him to develop a style in which everything
but the essential line was discarded, the secret behind his brilliant
simplicity and vividness of character. His chalk study of Henry Irving
(page 105) is one of the Club's most cherished possessions and his
self-portrait (page 106) could scarcely be more economical in its
draughtsmanship. One carping critic (none other than W. G. Grace) once
reproachfully asked him in a telegram: 'Why, oh why, does square-leg
wear wicket-keeping gloves?' A reply telegram helpfully explained:

SAVAGE CLUB
HOUSE DINNER
ALAN BROCK in the CHAIR
Sat. November 5th 1949
1 CARLTON HOUSE TERRACE · S·W·1

'To keep his hands warm'.

Both Bertie Meyer (page 107) and José Levy (page 108) were theatre proprietors (St Martin's Theatre and The Little Theatre). Bertie was honoured on his ninetieth birthday with a special dinner at which the newest and youngest Savage, Joe Brown, took the Chair (page 109). Always a generous soul, and always immaculately dressed with a trimming of diamond studs, Bertie presented the Club with the glittering Waterford chandeliers that illuminated the dining-room at Carlton House Terrace. When someone enquired where these had come from, he was told: 'From Bertie Meyer, he got tired of wearing them.'

If the scientists seem to have had a thin time in this gallery, it is mainly, I think, because there is less exhibitionism in them than in the rest of us They were, you recall, introduced to give 'a leavening of seriousness into the Bohemian levity'. Not that Magnus Pyke (page 110), encompassed with bags of faith, sawdust, gravel, hope, and gravity and concocting a witch's brew, looks a model of seriousness; nor, for that matter, does Sir Walter Perry, Vice-Chancellor of the Open University (page 111). In general, however, these brethren prefer to be enigmatic, like the explorer Nansen (page 112), or self-effacing like Robert Falcon Scott (page 113). That doesn't prevent some of them becoming skittish. Witness the occasion when our Nobel Prize-winning physicist, Professor R. G. W Norrish, manufactured a toy bomb – intended to create a diversion in the card-room – confused the ingredients, and blew out the windows instead.

Their spirit of irreverence may be less extrovert than that of, for example, Billy Leonard (page 114), who professionally was a pantomime dame and recreationally the Club jester. (Unfortunately too many of Billy's jests depend on the ambience of an instant and appear flatfooted and clumsy in print.) Nevertheless, in the matter of marvellously informative, if sometimes esoteric, conversation, they stand their corner, as the saying has it. On my first visit to the Club as a probationary Member, I was accompanied by my proposer, Macdonald Hastings. Anxious to see that I didn't put a foot wrong, he warned me that I had better not venture into conversational realms which were not my country As anxious as he to keep my probationary slate clean, I assured him I wouldn't. 'I can always talk about the weather', I said glibly. 'For God's

Savage Club
House Dinner
April 11th
1953
GUY'S NIGHT
IN THE CHAIR: GUY BOUSFIELD

sake don't do that', he said. 'You may well find yourself sitting next
to the world's most eminent meteorological expert.'

The probationary period – to clarify matters – is a long-established
safeguard against unhappy integration. Before Members are actually
elected, they are invited on a specific date to meet the Committee and
to use the Club as 'candidates' for a month. If at the end of that month
no one has detected any reason against it, the candidature is consummated
by election. It gives both sides a chance to opt out without hard feelings
or embarrassment, ensures as far as it is possible to do so that everyone
is at home with everyone else, and puts a final inner door on the Club's
exclusiveness.

One of the most ardent sentries at that door is Matthew Norgate, no
less, the compiler of this book and occasional Chairman of the
Qualifications Committee, which considers, extremely solemnly, every
nomination submitted before it is even glimpsed by the General Committee.

The first of the card-night menus on page 115 shows this exemplar of
Club rectitude sitting on the extreme left of the poker table, younger and
handsomer than he is now, and wearing a halo, which has been
conspicuously absent on the many occasions I've been in his company.
A shy man, this is the only example of his several House Dinner
chairmanships he has chosen to put in this book. For the record, the
others at the table are (reading clockwise from Matthew): Mark
Hambourg, Charles Dorning, Moore Raymond, Victor MacClure,
Douglas Furber, George Whitelaw (many of whose drawings may be
seen in these pages), Benno Moiseiwitsch, Sir Louis Sterling, George Wood,
and Kennedy Russell. Victor MacClure, by the way, drew the extremely
effective Annual Dinner card on page 116 to celebrate the occasion when
C. E. Lawrence, the Honorary Secretary of the time, took the Chair to
welcome Sir John Martin-Harvey as the Club's Guest of Honour.
Another incidental, and almost redundant, piece of information: the
smiler with the hammer and chisel on page 117, Marcus Paterson, was a
Club Honorary Treasurer from 1923 to 1931.

This is almost where we came in, with that laconic remark about the
subscription being whatever Members chose to owe. It isn't of course,
though the notorious fluctuations of the artist's income at times
contradict that assertion. The anachronistic nature of clubs in a hell-bent

SAVAGE CLUB HOUSE DINNER

MARCH 11, 1922.   FRED GORLE IN THE CHAIR

62

world may force the less principled institutions to adopt such devious and desperate measures as amalgamation with other clubs, removal to smaller premises, the sales of cherished possessions at Sotheby's or Christie's, or the calling in of property developers to make fantastic offers for freeholds. Not so the Savage – it hasn't raised its subscription in a decade, sold its soul by amalgamation, called in the property men (it's never had a freehold to sell anyway), or let slip its tenacious hold on exclusiveness of Membership.

The Club contrives, with a great deal of native cunning, an unpaid Executive, and a minuscule staff (specifically, four), to keep its autonomy, its character, and its cool. The pursuit of happiness, by way of the Savage Club, continues.

Tom Purvis

Savage Club
Saturday September 25
1926

FRED-H-GORLE IN THE *CHAIR —
* QUERY BARBER'S OR ELECTRIC — ANY WAY
— HEAVEN HELP THE BARBER ON A NIGHT LIKE THIS!

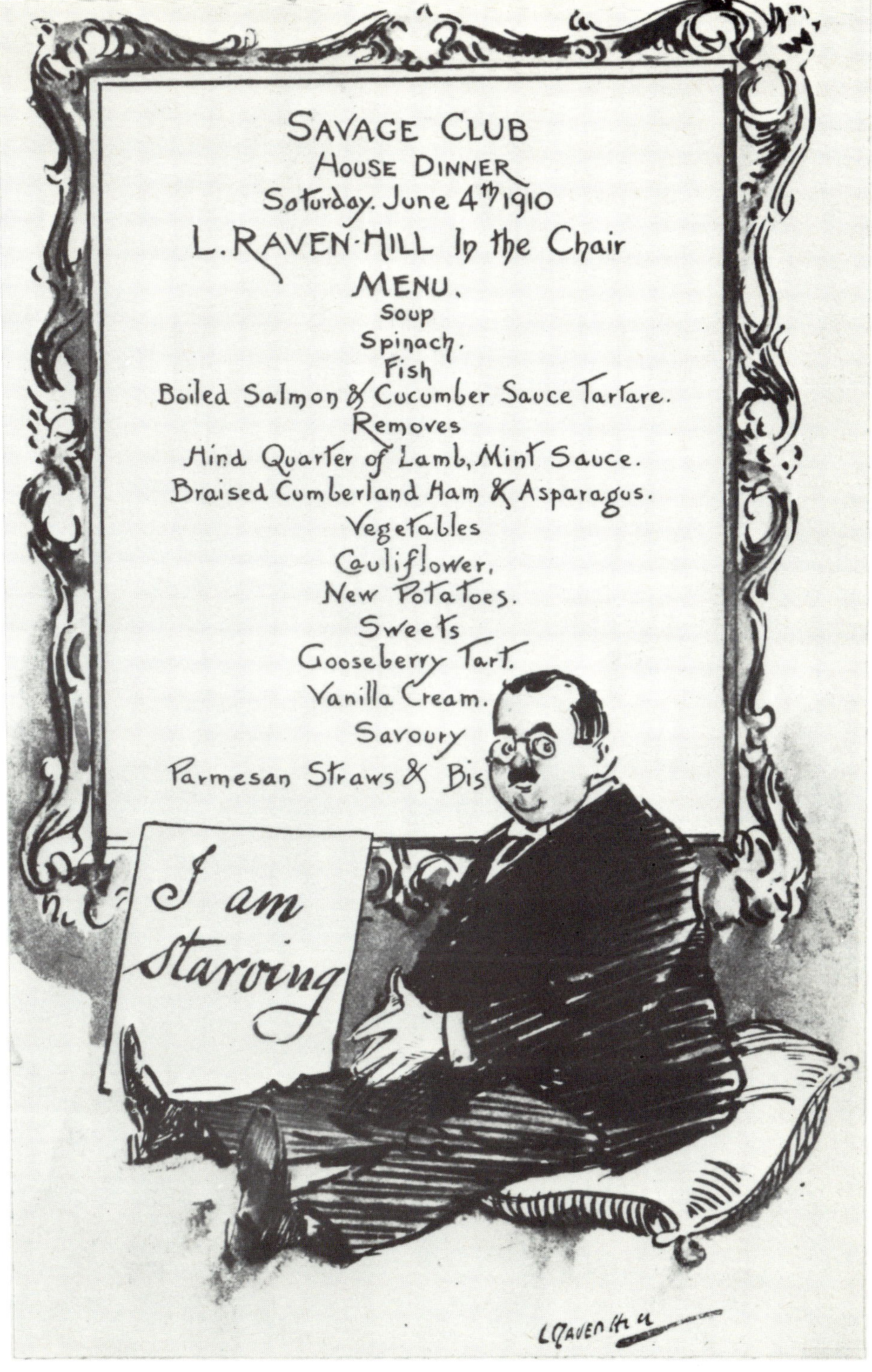

SAVAGE CLUB
HOUSE DINNER
Saturday. June 4th 1910
L. RAVEN-HILL In the Chair
MENU.
Soup
Spinach.
Fish
Boiled Salmon & Cucumber Sauce Tartare.
Removes
Hind Quarter of Lamb, Mint Sauce.
Braised Cumberland Ham & Asparagus.
Vegetables
Cauliflower,
New Potatoes.
Sweets
Gooseberry Tart.
Vanilla Cream.
Savoury
Parmesan Straws & Bis
I am Starving

SAVAGE CLUB
HOUSE DINNER
FEB 10TH 1923
L. RAVEN HILL
in the
Chair
YACHTING
WORLD
"NOW BERTIE NO FLATTERY."
"RIGHTO RAVEN"

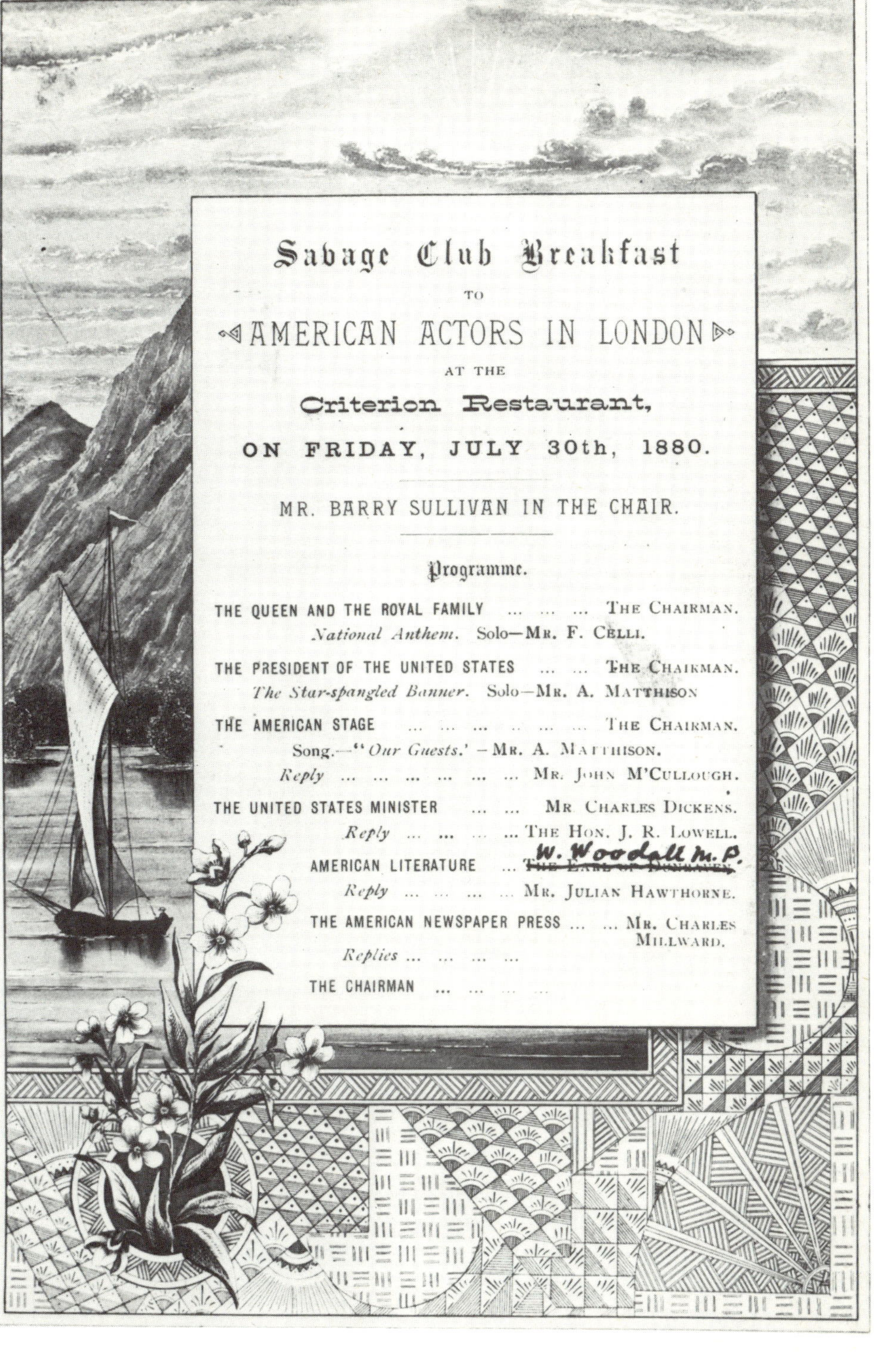

Savage Club Breakfast
TO
◁ AMERICAN ACTORS IN LONDON ▷
AT THE
Criterion Restaurant,
ON FRIDAY, JULY 30th, 1880.

MR. BARRY SULLIVAN IN THE CHAIR.

Programme.

THE QUEEN AND THE ROYAL FAMILY ... ... THE CHAIRMAN.
National Anthem. Solo—MR. F. CELLI.

THE PRESIDENT OF THE UNITED STATES ... ... THE CHAIRMAN.
The Star-spangled Banner. Solo—MR. A. MATTHISON

THE AMERICAN STAGE ... ... THE CHAIRMAN.
Song.—"Our Guests.'—MR. A. MATTHISON.
Reply ... ... MR. JOHN M'CULLOUGH.

THE UNITED STATES MINISTER ... ... MR. CHARLES DICKENS.
Reply ... ...THE HON. J. R. LOWELL.
AMERICAN LITERATURE ... THE EARL OF DUNRAVEN.
Reply ... ... MR. JULIAN HAWTHORNE.

THE AMERICAN NEWSPAPER PRESS ... ... MR. CHARLES
MILLWARD.
Replies ... ...

THE CHAIRMAN ... ...

SAVAGE CLUB
HOUSE DINNER
JULY 6.
1907

MENU
Soup
MOCK TURTLE
FISH
TURBOT
Sauce Hollandaise
REMOVES
HIND QUARTER of LAMB
MINT SAUCE
ROAST DUCKLING
& GREEN PEAS
SWEETS
FRUIT JELLIES
CHARLOTTE à la RUSSE
SAVOURY
SOFT ROES on TOAST

Mark Twain

SIR JAMES D. LINTON. R.I
IN THE CHAIR
WELCOME TO
MARK TWAIN

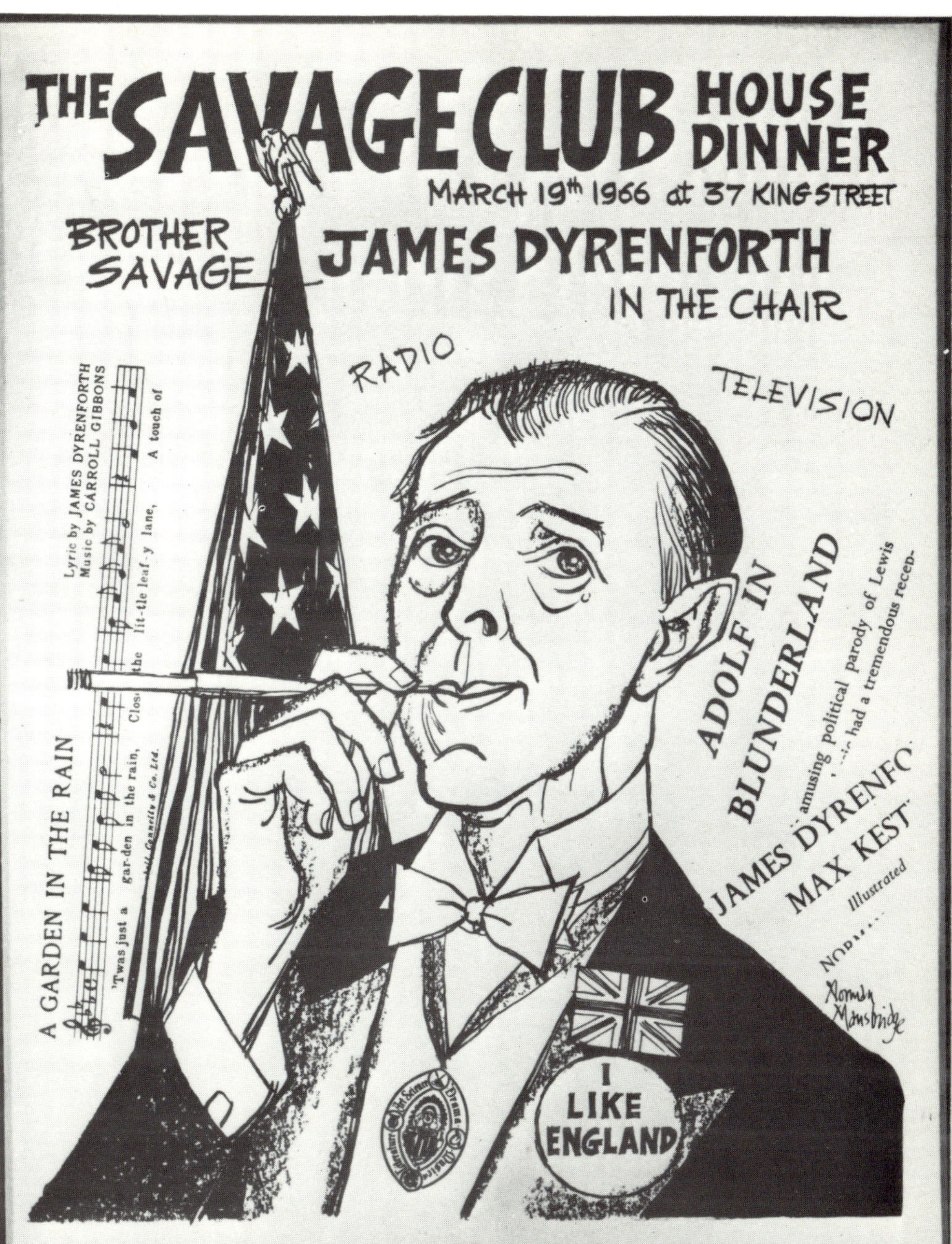
THE SAVAGE CLUB HOUSE DINNER
MARCH 19th 1966 at 37 KING STREET
BROTHER SAVAGE
JAMES DYRENFORTH
IN THE CHAIR
RADIO
TELEVISION
Lyric by JAMES DYRENFORTH
Music by CARROLL GIBBONS
A GARDEN IN THE RAIN
A touch of
the lit-tle leaf-y lane,
Clos
the
'Twas just a gar-den in the rain,
ADOLF IN
BLUNDERLAND
amusing political parody of Lewis
had a tremendous recep-
JAMES DYRENFO
MAX KEST
Illustrated
I LIKE ENGLAND
Norman
Mansbridge

Section of Rachmaninoff Concerto Rehearsal at the Queen's Hall.
Benno Moiseiwitsch in the Chair.

SAVAGE CLUB
84th ANNUAL DINNER
George Baker in the Chair
Guest of the Club
His Excellency the
Ambassador to the
Court of St. James
from the U·S·S·R
M·IVAN
MAISKY
Harry Riley
SCIENCE
ART
DRAMA
LITERATURE
MUSIC
Saturday · December 6th · 1941

UMM... MAH...

SAVAGE CLUB
ANNUAL DINNER

Brother Savage HARRY RILEY in the Chair

Guest of the Club

SIR CHARLES WHEELER KCVO. CBE. PRA.

Menu
Fillet of Sole Walewska
Chicken Sauté Chasseur
Brioche Potatoes + Cauliflower
Scotch Woodcock + Coffee

3 DECEMBER 1960.   1 CARLTON HOUSE TERRACE S.W.I.

SAVAGE CLUB LADIES' NIGHT
June 20 1969
at 86 St James's Street
S.W.1.
GUEST OF HONOUR
IN THE CHAIR
BASIL BOOTHROYD
THE OBSERVER REVIEW.
KATHARINE WHITEHORN
THE DAILY ROUND
MENU
Orange & Grapefruit Cocktail
Consommé Julienne
Poached Salmon
Sauce Hollandaise
Buttered Peas
New Potatoes
Strawberry Flan & Cream
Coffee
John Worsley

Savage Club
Ladies' Night
1953

At the Park Lane Hotel
on Sunday, May 10th, 1953.
+ + +
Guest of the Evening,
Dame Edith Evans, D.B.E.
+ + +
In the Chair; Brother
Savage Alec H. Nash.
+ + +

A recollection of our Guest of the Evening in
her memorable portrayal of the Nurse in 'Romeo and Juliet' at the New
Theatre. October 1935.

SHERRIFS
/1953

'MR. H.,
1952

'TOMMY.

SAVAGE CLUB
annual XCII dinner
on Saturday, 3rd December, 1949
at Carlton House Terrace.
In the chair: Guest of the club:
SIR ALAN   COMPTON
HERBERT,   MACKENZIE,
M.P.   O.B.E.

CUMHA   DO DH'UILLEAM
SISEAL?   SPAIDSEARACHD
DHUIC PHEAIRT? STAD
CHREAG EALACHAIDH?
AH'M SORRY SURR
BUT AH DO NOT KEN
WHIT YE ARE
SAYING.

SAVAGE CLUB HOUSE DINNER
Bro/Sav.
JACK TRAIN
in the Chair
Feb. 4th 1956
"Colonel Chinstrop I presume!"
Riley

Savage Club House Dinner
at King Street
20th November 1965
GOOD ON YER, SPORT
By George, he's got it!
By George, he's got it!
GEORGE SPROD
in the Chair
ffolkes

From the Illustrated London News. By Harry Furniss.

THE 77TH ANNUAL DINNER OF THE SAVAGE CLUB
December. 1st 1934.
THEY'RE ALL A LOT OF HEATHEN 'SO DON'T DON'T BOX CLEVER 'SAH - JUST GIVE 'EM A 'BELT WITH THIS 'ERE GAVEL.
TOM WEBSTER 34.
H.R.H. the Duke of York IN THE CHAIR.

SAVAGE CLUB DINNER
MENU.
THICK MOCK TURTLE.
BOILED SALMON.
TARTARE SAUCE
ROAST BEEF
SPINACH.
COMPOTE OF FRUIT.
FRENCH FINGER PASTRIES.
CHEESE.
CAPT J. BELL WHITE
IN THE CHAIR
SAT 2ND OF JUNE
ART
SCIENCE
THE DRAMA
HISTORY
SAILING
U.S.A.
TO WELCOME OUR NEW BROTHER SAVAGE ADMIRAL SIR JOHN JELLICOE. G.C.B. G.C.V.O. O.M.

SAVAGE CLUB
HOUSE DINNER
OCT 28TH 1933
WOOD
in the Chair.
THE NAUGHTY NINETIES
AND SO ON

SAVAGE CLUB
An address of Welcome to the American and Australian Guests of the Savage
by Will E. Chapman
NORTH QUEENS LAND.
Dudley Hardy. 86.
W. B. WHITTINGHAM & Co 91 GRACECHURCH ST LONDON. E.C.

SAVAGE CLUB
HOUSE DINNER
MAY 3RD 1924
LEON M
ALBREY HAMMOND. (with apologies to the WEMBLEY LION)
IN THE CHAIR

SAVAGE CLUB
SEPT. 14th 1894.
ODELL'S EIGHTIETH BIRTHDAY.
ED. CLEARY. CHAIR.
NOT YET OLD CHAP
MENU.
SOUP.
CLEAR MOCK TURTLE.
THICK
FISH
SALMON. LOBSTER SAUCE
STEWED EELS.
FRIED WHITING
ENTRÉE.
FRICASSEED. SWEETBREADS
SAVOUREY RISSOLES
JOINTS.
SIRLOIN BEEF
HORSE RADISH SAUCE
BOILED LEG OF MUTTON
SWEETS.
PINE APPLE PUDDING.
COMPOTE OF DAMSONS
STEWED PEACHES.
WHIPPED CREAM.
VARIOUS JELLIES

SAVAGE
CLUB
HOUSE DINNER
Saturday
December 7th 1918
ALBERT TOFT
IN THE CHAIR
VICTORY!
ONE MUST DO SOMETHING TILL 6.30

"Brothers, you all are here, we trust,
For none should miss to-night's great BUST"
Shakespeare

SAVAGE CLUB HOUSE DINNER
ENGLISH NIGHT— Saturday, 24th April, 1926.
CHARLEY HANDS IN THE CHAIR
GUEST OF THE CLUB, ALBERT TOFT

MENU
SOUP
HARE
FISH
TURBOT MAÎTRE D'HOTEL
REMOVES
HAUNCH OF MUTTON
RED CURRANT JELLY
ROAST PHEASANT & CHIPS
BREAD SAUCE
VEGETABLES
BRUSSELS SPROUTS
GRILLED TOMATOES
POTATOES
SWEETS
COMPÔTE OF APRICOTS
VANILLA CREAM
SAVOURY
SOFT ROES ON TOAST
SAVAGE CLUB
HOUSE DINNER
DEC 5th 1908
MAX PEMBERTON
IN THE CHAIR

DON RAFAEL →
NOV 24TH
1923
SAVAGE CLUB
HOUSE DINNER
RAFAEL SABATINI
in the Chair

SAVAGE CLUB
HOUSE DINNER
OCT. 16TH 1926.
EDGAR WALLACE IN THE CHAIR
THE SINISTER MAN
EDGAR
W—WHAT WAS THA . . ?

SAVAGE CLUB
HOUSE DINNER
DEC. 6th 1919
BART KENNEDY
IN THE CHAIR

TAKING A CORRESPONDENCE COURSE WITH THE CHAIRMAN — PERCY. V. BRADSHAW.

HEIL
NAZI NIGHT
Savage Club
HOUSE DINNER · JAN 5TH 1935
Percy Von Bradshaw
IN THE CHAIR

LEONARDO DA VINCI MIGHT HAVE DRAWN THIS MENU FOR ME BUT HE SEEMS TO HAVE LEFT HIS OLD ADDRESS

I KNOW VANDYCK WOULD HAVE VOLUNTEERED BUT I COULD'NT GET HIM ON THE PHONE.

VELASQUEZ WOULD HAVE LOVED TO DO IT, BUT HE'S DEAD.

MICHAELANGELO SUFFERS FROM THE SAME COMPLAINT

AND SO DOES HOGARTH

JOHN SAYS HE HAS THE TIME, BUT NOT THE ABILITY.

SAVAGE CLUB HOUSE DINNER SAT. APRIL 28, 1928

ME IN THE CHAIR

ORPEN SAYS VICE VERSA.

AUBREY HAMMOND IS AWAY — AND SO —

I HAVE HAD TO DRAW THE DARN THING MYSELF!

SAVAGE CLUB HOUSE DINNER
November 19th 1921
George Stampa in the chair

98

THE SAVAGE CLUB

91st. ANNUAL DINNER
B. C. HILLIAM IN THE CHAIR

Guest of the Club: The Right Hon. Mr. Justice Birkett.

SATURDAY   DECEMBER   4th., 1948

The 99th ANNUAL DINNER of THE SAVAGE CLUB 1956
Guest of Honour
THE LORD CHIEF JUSTICE OF ENGLAND
LORD GODDARD of ALDBOURNE
with
Brother Savage
REGINALD POUND
in the Chair
December 1st
"....POUND FOR POUND......"
Harry Windslade
Menu
Goujons of Turbot
Tartar Sauce
Fricassee of Chicken
with Red Wine Sauce
Buttered Small Peas · Duchesse Potatoes
Canapé Convert
Coffee

102

SAVAGE CLUB
HOUSE DINNER
MARCH 28TH
1925
MENU
Mock Turtle Soup
Braised Turbot Sonchet
Roast Sirloin of Beef
Yorkshire Pudding
Horse Raddish Sce
Roast Potatoes
Spinach
Biscuits, Cheese, Butter.
Coffee
IN THE CHAIR

THE
SAVAGE
CLUB
FEB·12
1938
THEODORE
HOLLAND
IN THE
CHAIR
SIR JAMES JEANS
THE GUEST OF THE
EVENING
PROTONS
XENON
PHOTONS
OZONE
ELECTRON
PROTONS
ATOMS
LIUM
ETHER
W HEATH
ROBINSON
AN EARLY ATTEMPT TO SPLIT THE ATOM

SIR HENRY IRVING AS MEPHISTOPHELES.

(*A "lightning sketch" by* PHIL MAY.)

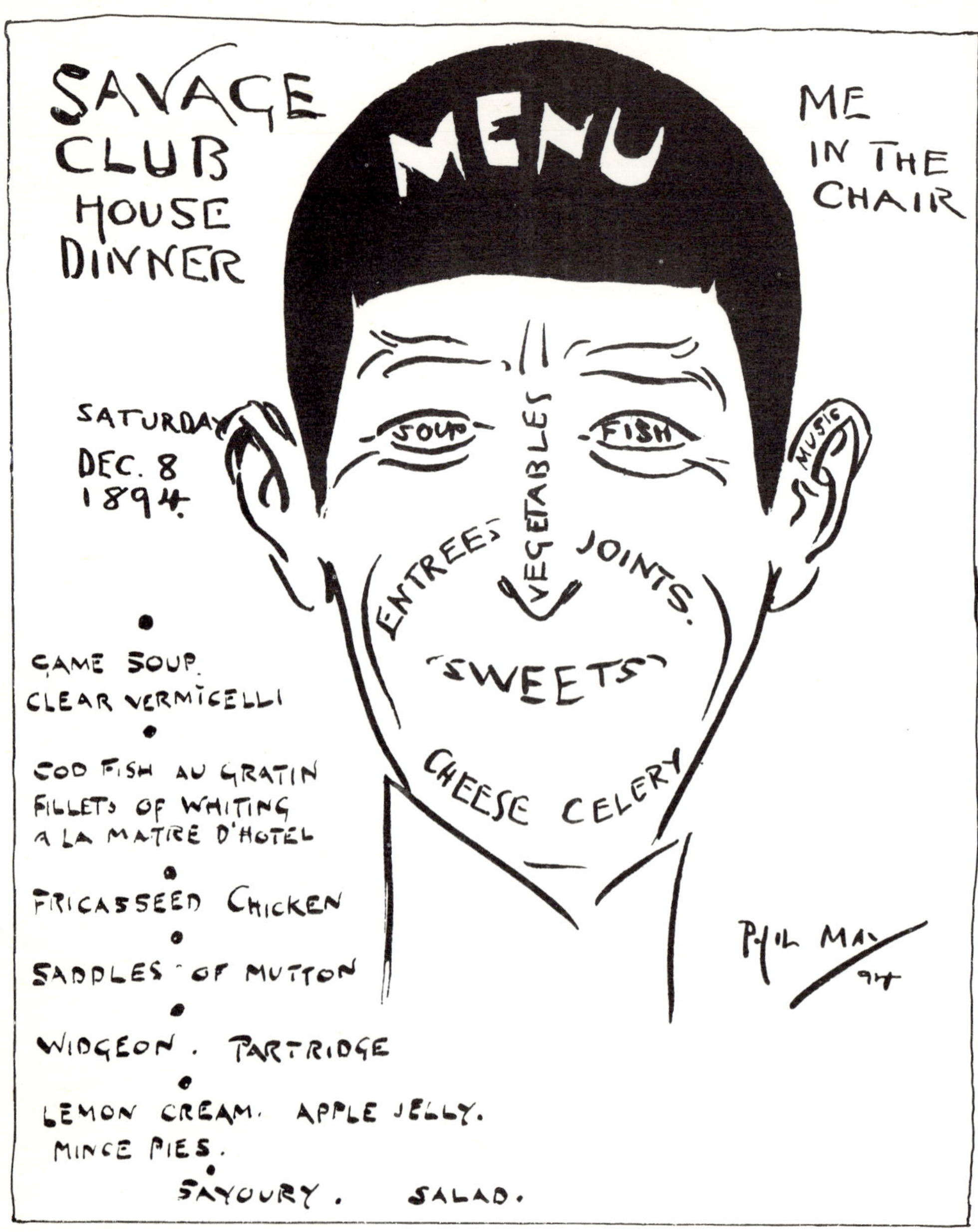

MENU
SAVAGE CLUB HOUSE DINNER
ME IN THE CHAIR
SOUP
VEGETABLES
FISH
MUSIC
ENTREES
JOINTS.
"SWEETS"
CHEESE CELERY
SATURDAY DEC. 8 1894.
GAME SOUP.
CLEAR VERMICELLI
COD FISH AU GRATIN
FILLETS OF WHITING A LA MAITRE D'HOTEL
FRICASSEED CHICKEN
SADDLES OF MUTTON
WIDGEON. PARTRIDGE
LEMON CREAM. APPLE JELLY.
MINCE PIES.
SAVOURY. SALAD.
PHIL MAY 94

AUBREY HAMMOND. quelques kilomètres d'après Remisoff, Soudeikine, benoit

PORTRAIT OF A MAN WITH BLACK·HAIR

SAVAGE CLUB HOUSE DINNER FEB 25TH 1928

JOSÉ LEVY IN THE CHAIR

SAVAGE CLUB
HOUSE DINNER
IN THE CHAIR
BROTHER SAVAGE
JOE BROWN
6 months a Savage!
JUNE 18 1967
AT 31 KING STREET COVENT GARDEN W.C.2.
Charlie Girl
HONOURED GUEST OF THE CLUB
BERTIE MEYER
90 years of age yesterday!
60 years a savage!
MENU
Eggs in Aspic
Roast Saddle of Lamb
Red current Jelly
Buttered Peas
New Potatoes
Strawberry Melba
Coffee

MULLIGATAWNY
BOILED LEG OF MUTTON
CAPER SAUCE
CREAMED POTATOES
GARDEN PEAS
WELSH RABBIT
COFFEE
SAVAGE CLUB HOUSE DINNER
AT
86 St JAMES ST SW.1
FEB 15 1974
Nutritional adviser
Dr MAGNUS PYKE
FRSE
BAAS
?
FAITH
SAWDUST
GRAVEL
HOPE
GRAVITY
SCOTCH MIST
KW.

SAVAGE CLUB
HOUSE DINNER
in the chair
Bro. Savage
Dr WALTER LAING MACDONALD PERRY
OBE. MD. DSc. FRCPE. FRSE
Vice-Chancellor of the Open University
Friday 3rd March 1972
at 86
St James's
Street S.W.1
CVRRIKVLVM
ENROLMENT:
(prep.) Oxtail Soup
TVTORIALS:
(Subjects for digestion)
Hungarian Beef Goulash
Macaire Potatoes
Buttered Carrots
EXAMS:
Quiche Lorraine
RESVLTS: Coffee
Anthony Gray

"A SAVAGE CLUB SOUVENIR."

SAVAGE CLUB
HOUSE DINNER
Capt. R.F. Scott
IN THE CHAIR
JUNE 10
1909
WELCOME TO LIEUT. E. H. SHACKLETON
MENU
SOUP
Spinach
Seaweed
FISH
Scott Salmon
& Cucumber
Sauce tartare
to South Pole
REMOVES
Hind quarter
of Lamb
Sleigh dog
Mint Sauce
Duckling
Roast penguin
& green peas
VEGETABLES
Moss Lichen
Cabbage &
new potatoes
SWEETS
Fruit Jellyfish
Antartic
Coffee Cream
70° below
SAVORY
Seals eggs
& Kipper on
toast.

Savage Club House Dinner
Oct. 1st 1955
George Baker
in the Chair
Guest of the Club..
BILLY LEONARD
1 CARLTON HOUSE TERRACE · · · · · S.W.1
Riley

Henry Riley
MENU
Les Huîtres or
Grape Fruit Frappe
Creme St. Germain
Salmon Hollandaise
Pommes Nouvelles
Petits Pois
Glacé Tutti-Frutti
Cafe
SAVAGE CLUB HOUSE DINNER
April 1st · 1950 · "CARDS NIGHT"
MATTHEW NORGATE in the Chair
1 CARLTON HOUSE TERRACE · S·W·1

SAVAGE CLUB SATURDAY, DECEMBER 3
81st. ANNUAL DINNER 1938
In the Chair: C.E. LAWRENCE
Sir JOHN MARTIN-HARVEY
HOTEL VICTORIA
Guest of the Club
THE SHADE: "AND SO, MY SAVAGE BRETHREN,
- YOU STILL CARE TO HONOUR A
PLAYER!"
VICTOR MACCLURE

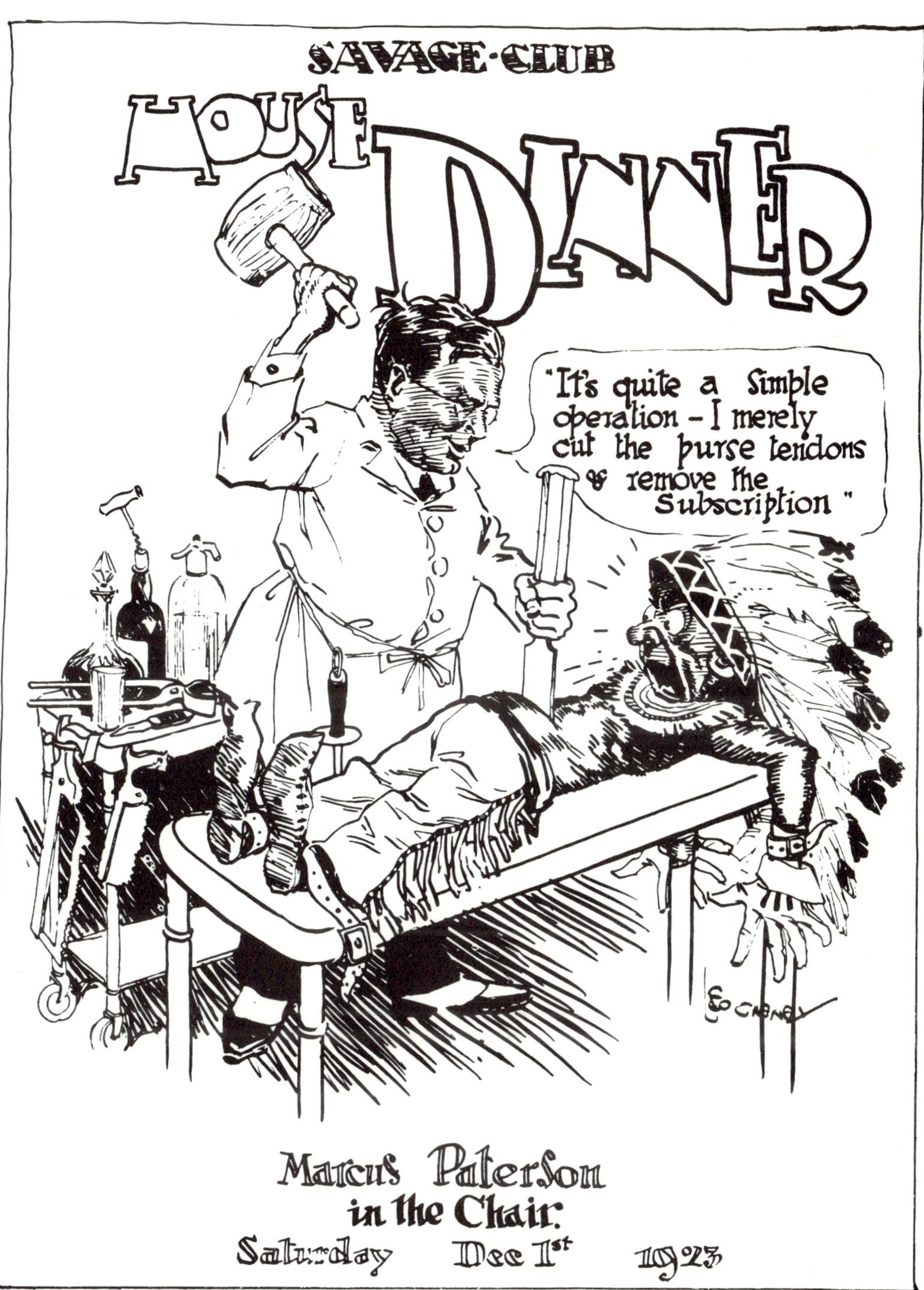

SAVAGE·CLUB
HOUSE DINNER
"It's quite a Simple operation - I merely cut the purse tendons & remove the Subscription"
Marcus Paterson in the Chair.
Saturday   Dec 1st   1923

Savage Miscellany

Another Prince of Wales (Edward VIII), whose feathers look as if they have been hurriedly borrowed from the headdress of a duchess at a débutantes' ball.

Judging by the lists of toasts and entertainers (Phil May and Brandon Thomas among them) the 38th anniversary dinner must have gone on pretty well all night. That's Henry Irving being histrionic on the right.

Australians must get awfully tired of being continually decorated with symbolic kangaroos, and of the down-under, upside-down joke. The Duke of Gloucester, who later became Governor-General, was made an Honorary Life Member at this dinner and forswore ever to topsy-turvy in a speech.

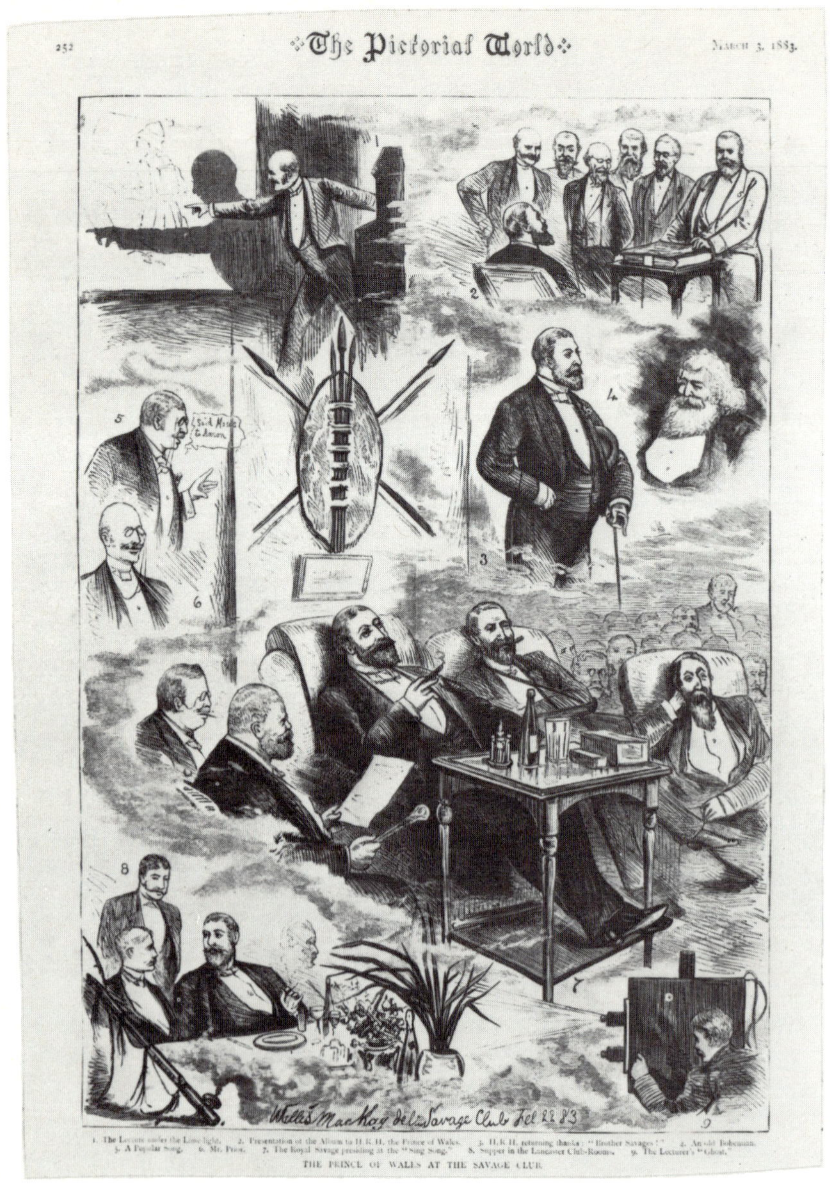

THE PRINCE OF WALES AT THE SAVAGE CLUB.

1. The Lecture under the Lime-light.   2. Presentation of the Album to H.R.H. the Prince of Wales.   3. H.R.H. returning thanks: "Brother Savages!"   4. An old Bohemian.   5. A Popular Song.   6. Mr. Frost.   7. The Royal Savage presiding at the "Sing-Song."   8. Supper in the Lancaster Club-Room.   9. The Lecturer's "Ghost."

The Savage with his feet under the table is the Prince of Wales, and he is said in the caption to be 'Presiding at the Sing-Song'. The deputation in the top right-hand corner is presenting him with a souvenir album.

122

The fiftieth anniversary dinner at the Hotel Cecil was attended by 344 Members and guests. Sir Charles Wyndham was the theatrical impressario and theatre owner (Criterion, Wyndham's etc), and the menu artist was Lawson Wood. Several racist cracks ('Foot it, Sambo or we shall miss de *hors d'oeuvre*' for example) are included; but these were not thought offensive then.

These two self-drawn Aubrey Hammond cards demonstrate that he was a big man who got bigger with time; also that he was an extremely good artist.

SAVAGE CLUB
HOUSE DINNER
APRIL 26TH
1924
BING!
MENU
-
Potage Bonne Femme
-
Brill. Tomato Sauce
-
Roast Sirloin of Beef
Yorkshire Pudding
Horseradish Sauce
Pommes Boulangére
Spinach
-
Pêche Melba.
-
Café
AUBREY HAMMOND
IN THE CHAIR

Dancing girls don't often appear in the Savage; but they were justifiably depicted behind Harry Randall, pop star and song writer of the inter-war years.

Harry Tate of the still lingeringly famous 'Golfing' and 'Motoring' sketches, had a fruity voice and an indomitable command of English (and of Scotch, come to that). It is on record in the Minutes that 'a hundred diners sat down but there were seats for only 92'. This mystery is not further explained.

There is little to be said about this fortieth anniversary dinner except that, with all those entertainers and all those toasts, it must have gone on for a very long time.

This charming pastoral scene has no detectable Savage significance. It's
just a charming pastoral scene by Yeend (a unique name, surely?) King,
bosom buddy of Dudley Hardy, who drew the Tom Marlowe card also
reproduced herein.

Two more perfect examples of Aubrey Hammond's characteristic style.

SAVAGE CLUB
LADIES' NIGHT
MAY 7TH 1939
LORD PETER VIEWS the BODY
AUBREY HAMMOND
or
"A Gaudy Night"
IN THE CHAIR
HUBERT HARBEN
GUEST of the CLUB
MISS
DOROTHY · L · SAYERS

G. A. Henty had (and probably still has) a tremendous following for
his boys' adventure stories, all of which featured clean-limbed action
and glowing cheeks. But he was also a distinguished war correspondent
for the *Daily Telegraph* and a Trustee of the Club. In the smaller card
the correspondents being welcomed home are Herbert Johnson, Hilary
Skinner, J. M. Le Sage, Bennet Burleigh, and J. A. Cameron.

SAVAGE CLUB
LADIES' NIGHT
DINNER AT THE
HOTEL CECIL
SATURDAY. MAY 3rd 1902
G. A. HENTY
IN THE
CHAIR
W.D.ALMOND

133

Edwin Evans the great music critic was a staunch proponent of Elgar's music. In his note for the memorial concert given after Elgar's death in 1934 he said: 'In his works music held her head high.'

Captain Walter Kirton wrote extensively about China in the *National Review*, of which he was owner and editor.

SAVAGE CLUB LADIES' NIGHT

JUNE 18th 1971 at 86 St JAMES'S STREET S.W.I.

IN THE CHAIR: BROTHER SAVAGE **ANTHONY HERN**

GUEST OF HONOUR: **LADY ANTONIA FRASER**

Anthony Hern is the Literary Editor of the *Evening Standard* and its Wine Correspondent too. At the time of writing he is also Chairman of the Savage Club's Committee.

Barrie lived nearby in Adelphi but wasn't a clubbable man. But apparently his evening as the Club's guest was an immense success.

This beautifully drawn and stylistically unique card is by Heath
Robinson, whose eccentric machinery, which he has temporarily deserted
here to touch with his magic the celebration of a Brother Savage's
occasion, is still the cause of great delight to its beholders.

Fantasy indeed. And this was in the days before girlie magazines.

Joe Simpson, whose self-portrait can be seen elsewhere, had the knack of depicting character with a marvellous economy of line, as here.

Arnold Ridley's world-famous *Ghost Train* first steamed across the stage in 1925. At the time of writing he's appearing nightly (plus matinees) in London in a staged version of *Dad's Army*, which isn't bad for a man pushing eighty. Besides the *Train* he's had twenty-seven other plays produced, has written and directed films, and become a much loved personality of television and wireless.

Appendix

THIS is not, one might have thought, the sort of book to have an
Appendix. Appendices usually trail along behind books with solemn
titles like *The Treatment and Disposal of Industrial Waste Water.*
But it seemed worth making an exception in the case of Mr Tegetmeier.
Mr Tegetmeier was one of my predecessors as Honorary Secretary –
specifically from 1859 to 1865. After which, I see it says in the Minutes,
he 'retired full of years and honour'. Nonsense. About the years, anyway.
He lived till 1912; and in 1900, on his birthday, gave all Savages a free
copy of his reminiscences of the Club, which he had privately printed.
Hence the Appendix to reproduce it in. As you will see, it has
considerable period charm.

REMINISCENCES

OF

THE SAVAGE CLUB

Presented to its Members

BY

W. B. TEGETMEIER,

November 10th, 1900.

REMINISCENCES

THE SAVAGE CLUB.

ON the occasion of presiding at the weekly dinner of the Savage Club, as the oldest living member of the Club, and as having been jointly with Andrew Halliday one of its first secretaries, I have thought it would be more acceptable to those who have done me the honour of attending to celebrate my eighty-fourth birthday to present them, in lieu of the usual ornamental *menu* with which they are familiar, with a few reminiscences of the Club, drawn by many of its artistic members.

These drawings had their beginning in the following circumstance: Thirty years ago I chanced in the Club to be reading Tennyson's "In Memoriam," when Frank Vizitelly, who died recently, it is supposed, in the wilds of the Soudan, came to bid his fellow members farewell, and I asked him to sign his name on one of the numerous blank spaces of the book. He did so, and, having the name of one member of the Savage Club, it occurred to me to use the volume as an autograph book, not only for the signatures of the members, but also for those of others of my friends and acquaintances. It contains the names of many of the most illustrious and esteemed of our scientific writers; Darwin's only pun, and Faraday's only complimentary autograph, appear in its pages, but the drawings by many of our fellow members here reproduced have reference either to the Club or to myself.

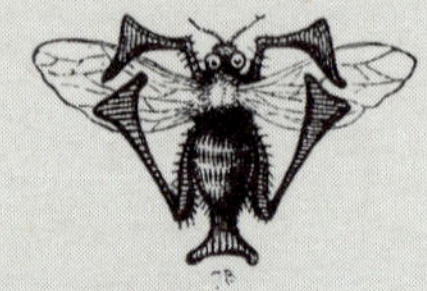

And made me that delirious man
Whose fancy fuses old and new,
And flashes into false and true,
And mingles all without a plan ?

THE above graceful drawing by Julian Portch stands solely on its own merits, without any reference to the lines it surrounds.

We keep the day.   With festal cheer,
With books and music, surely we
Will drink to him what e'er he be,
And sing the songs he loved to hear.

MAY I express the hope that these lines and the accompanying illustration of them, by our old Bohemian friend, Brunton, may be remembered on some future anniversary.

THE following beautiful illustration has a melancholy interest. Val Bromley and myself had had a slight misunderstanding. We were thoroughly reconciled, and he asked me to let him make a sketch in my book. The result was this graceful drawing of his wife—the last he ever made. He had even then contracted small-pox, of which he died in a few days.

And every thought breaks out a rose.

THE sketch by Paul Gray has from a similar cause the same sad interest as the last. We had been to the funeral of Morton, one of the most promising of the band of young artists who were then members of the Club; Gray was overwhelmed with grief at the loss of his friend. To divert his thoughts I begged him to make a sketch, and this is what he drew. It was also the last he ever made, for he, too, went home and died.

The recollection of our brother member, T. B. Hardy, is fresh in our memory. Making one of our party at whist, he cut out. Waiting for his turn to come into the next rubber, he asked for my book, and returned it before the termination of our game with the following addition :

EVERY member of the Club can still recall one of the original members, Edward Draper, who was for so many years our Honorary Solicitor. As an artist of the grotesque he was rarely surpassed. His sketch gives an admirable likeness of himself, when a young man, in close proximity to that of Ben Caunt, and is an apt illustration of the quotation.

Draper was celebrated for his extremely grotesque caricatures. I present an example, and leave it to others to identify the original.

MANY years since, when working with Darwin on " Variation in Animals," I was secretary to a Pigeon Club, whose meetings were held in Freemasons' Hall. At one of these John Brough was present, and made the above sketch of one of the varieties exhibited.

I have always been associated with birds—wild or domesticated—and Wallis Mackay's sketch illustrates my first appearance in an ornithological character.

SAVAGES AT HOME

THE same artist, in one of the comic papers of the day, drew a sketch of the "Savages at Home." It may amuse some of the members to find themselves or their friends among the company.

Wallis Mackay was a facile and fertile caricaturist, and my features seemed to lend themselves to his pencil. In the sketch with the tricycle I am represented as abducting the fair daughter of a farmer—a monstrous libel on my moral character.

To myself, one of the most grateful sketches in the book is the following drawn by my old friend, Harry Furniss, respecting which my modesty forbids me to say more.

THE graceful landscape which closes the selection is]from the hand of my dear old friend, Hawes Craven.   The portrait of myself is a reproduction of a photograph by Elliot and Fry, taken on my 82nd birthday—1898.

Printed by HORACE COX, Windsor House, Bream's Buildings, Chancery Lane, E.C.

158

Bibliography

THERE are several books about the Club, but alas they are all out of print. Second-hand copies sometimes reveal themselves in booksellers' shelves and catalogues.

Savage Club Papers, edited by Andrew Halliday, the Hon. Sec. of the day, and published by Tinsley in 1867. *Savage Club Papers: Second Series*, was published in 1868 (also by Tinsley) and a *Third Series*, edited by J. E. Muddock, was published by Hutchinson in 1897. These are collections of contributions – stories, verses, essays, drawings etc – by Savage Members.

The Savage Club by Aaron Watson, published by T. Fisher Unwin in 1907. This is the most substantial history of the Club.

Savage Club Souvenir. Another collection of contributions by Savages, privately printed in an edition of 500 copies in 1916, to celebrate Thomas Catling's 40th year as Honorary Auditor.

Brother Savages and Guests by Percy V. Bradshaw, published by W. H. Allen in 1957 to celebrate the centenary of the Club. An illustrated history.

Recollections of a Savage by Edwin A. Ward, published by Herbert Jenkins in 1923.

Reminiscences of the Savage Club, by W. B. Tegetmeier, sometime Hon. Sec. A privately printed pamphlet; reproduced in its entirety in the Appendix above.

The Club also gets many mentions in the various histories of London Club life, and in hundreds of articles that have appeared in magazines and newspapers.